SO-APO-593

NEW DIRECTIONS FOR TEACHING AND LEARNING

Robert J. Menges, *Northwestern University*
EDITOR-IN-CHIEF

Marilla D. Svinicki, *University of Texas, Austin*
ASSOCIATE EDITOR

370.015
Ac1r

Academic Service Learning: A Pedagogy of Action and Reflection

Robert A. Rhoads
Michigan State University

Jeffrey P. F. Howard
University of Michigan

EDITORS

LASELL COLLEGE LIBRARY
AUBURNDALE, MASS.

Number 73, Spring 1998

JOSSEY-BASS PUBLISHERS
San Francisco

ACADEMIC SERVICE LEARNING: A PEDAGOGY OF ACTION AND REFLECTION
Robert A. Rhoads, Jeffrey P. F. Howard (eds.)
New Directions for Teaching and Learning, no. 73
Robert J. Menges, Editor-in-Chief
Marilla D. Svinicki, Associate Editor

Copyright © 1998 Jossey-Bass Inc., Publishers, 350 Sansome Street, San Francisco, CA 94104.

All rights reserved. No part of this publication may be reproduced, stored in a retrieval system, or transmitted, in any form or by any means, electronic, mechanical, photocopying, recording, or otherwise, without the prior written permission of the publisher.

Microfilm copies of issues and articles are available in 16mm and 35mm, as well as microfiche in 105mm, through University Microfilms Inc., 300 North Zeeb Road, Ann Arbor, Michigan 48106–1346.

ISSN 0271–0633   ISBN 0-7879-4276-6

New Directions for Teaching and Learning is part of The Jossey-Bass Higher and Adult Education Series and is published quarterly by Jossey-Bass Inc., Publishers, 350 Sansome Street, San Francisco, California 94104–1342. Periodicals postage paid at San Francisco, California, and at additional mailing offices. Postmaster: Send address changes to New Directions for Teaching and Learning, Jossey-Bass Inc., Publishers, 350 Sansome Street, San Francisco, California 94104–1342.

New Directions for Teaching and Learning is indexed in College Student Personnel Abstracts, Contents Pages in Education, and Current Index to Journals in Education (ERIC).

Subscriptions cost $54.00 for individuals and $90.00 for institutions, agencies, and libraries. Prices subject to change.

Editorial correspondence should be sent to the editor-in-chief, Robert J. Menges, Northwestern University, Center for the Teaching Professions, 2115 North Campus Drive, Evanston, Illinois 60208–2610.

Cover photograph by Richard Blair/Color & Light © 1990.

www.josseybass.com

Printed in the United States of America on acid-free recycled paper containing 100 percent recovered waste paper, of which at least 20 percent is postconsumer waste.

CONTENTS

FROM THE SERIES EDITORS

About This Publication. Since 1980, *New Directions for Teaching and Learning* (*NDTL*) has brought a unique blend of theory, research, and practice to leaders in postsecondary education. NDTL sourcebooks strive not only for solid substance but also for timeliness, compactness, and accessibility.

The series has four goals: to inform readers about current and future directions in teaching and learning in postsecondary education, to illuminate the context that shapes these new directions, to illustrate these new directions through examples from real settings, and to propose ways in which these new directions can be incorporated into still other settings.

This publication reflects our view that teaching deserves respect as a high form of scholarship. We believe that significant scholarship is conducted not only by researchers who report results of empirical investigations but also by practitioners who share disciplined reflections about teaching. Contributors to *NDTL* approach questions of teaching and learning as seriously as they approach substantive questions in their own disciplines, and they deal not only with pedagogical issues but also with the intellectual and social context in which these issues arise. Authors deal on the one hand with theory and research and on the other with practice, and they translate from research and theory to practice and back again.

About This Volume. Providing opportunities for students to engage in community service—or even requiring it of them—is becoming more common at colleges and universities. Contributors to this issue of *New Directions for Teaching and Learning* emphasize the *learning* side of service. In their view, service learning and academic learning are inseparable. As the editors have said, "Academic service learning is not about the *addition* of service *to* learning but rather the *integration* of service *with* learning." Taken seriously, the concepts and practices discussed in these chapters will enhance the effectiveness of academic service learning in any field.

Robert J. Menges, *Editor-in-Chief*
Marilla D. Svinicki, *Associate Editor*

EDITORS' NOTES

In this volume, we contribute to what we believe is a movement whose time has come. Service learning, with an emphasis on active, experiential, collaborative, and community-oriented learning, is a pedagogical model that speaks to many of the teaching and learning concerns identified in scores of national reports and books published over the past two decades (Boyer, 1987; Fairweather, 1996; Wingspread Group, 1993; Study Group, 1984). Additionally, service learning, as an innovative pedagogical model, addresses fundamental issues related to the role of higher learning in fostering socially responsible and caring citizens, a concern raised in recent social and educational analyses (Barber, 1992; Bellah and others, 1991; Boyer, 1990; Coles, 1993; Rhoads, 1997; Tierney, 1993). Clearly, higher education has a key role to play in developing democratic citizens, and service learning offers a relevant pedagogical model.

In developing *Academic Service Learning: A Pedagogy of Action and Reflection*, we stress academic service learning tied directly to the formal curriculum through a specific course or program of study. Thus, we asked the authors to consider service learning as *a pedagogical model that intentionally integrates academic learning and relevant community service*. There are four key aspects to this definition and our view of academic service learning. First, the phrase "pedagogical model" suggests that service learning is first and foremost a mode for teaching. Second, the term "intentionally" captures the idea that there must be a planned effort by the instructor; service learning is not left to chance. Third, the word "integrates" highlights the notion that learning from service must be connected to classroom learning and theory in its broadest sense. Finally, "relevant" stresses that the community service placements must be connected to the course of study.

With the preceding in mind, we offer a brief overview of the volume. In Chapter One, Kathleen Maas Weigert reviews the meaning and salient issues of service learning. Chapter Two, by Ira Harkavy and Lee Benson, traces the theoretical roots of service learning. Jeffrey Howard addresses service learning as a pedagogical model in Chapter Three. Meta Mendel-Reyes (Chapter Four) next explores the role of service learning in citizenship education. In Chapter Five, Robert Rhoads examines the interconnections between multiculturalism and service learning. Following Rhoads, David Cooper details various processes for weaving together reading, writing, and reflection (Chapter Six). In Chapter Seven, Kenneth Reardon discusses action research as service learning. Dwight Giles and Janet Eyler examine the state of research on service learning in Chapter Eight. The relationship between service learning and faculty and organizational culture is reviewed by Kelly Ward in Chapter Nine. In Chapter Ten, Edward Zlotkowski offers a matrix for understanding the theoretical and pragmatic forces that give meaning to service learning. In the concluding chapter, Scott Dixon delineates additional service learning resources.

Robert A. Rhoads
Jeffrey P. F. Howard
Editors

References

Barber, B. R. *An Aristocracy of Everyone: The Politics of Education and the Future of America.* New York: Oxford University Press, 1992.

Bellah, R. N., Madsen, R., Sullivan, W. M., Swidler, A., and Tipton, S. M. *The Good Society.* New York: Vintage Books, 1991.

Boyer, E. L. *College: The Undergraduate Experience in America.* New York: HarperCollins, 1987.

Boyer, E. L. *Scholarship Reconsidered: Priorities of the Professoriate.* Princeton, N.J.: Carnegie Foundation for the Advancement of Teaching, 1990.

Coles, R. *The Call of Service: A Witness to Idealism.* Boston: Houghton Mifflin, 1993.

Fairweather, J. S. *Faculty Work and Public Trust: Restoring the Value of Teaching and Public Service in American Academic Life.* Needham Heights, Mass.: Allyn & Bacon, 1996.

Rhoads, R. A. *Community Service and Higher Learning: Explorations of the Caring Self.* Albany: State University of New York Press, 1997.

Study Group on the Conditions of Excellence in American Higher Education. *Involvement in Learning.* Washington, D.C.: National Institute of Education, 1984.

Tierney, W. G. *Building Communities of Difference: Higher Education in the 21st Century.* New York: Bergin & Garvey, 1993.

Wingspread Group on Higher Education. *An American Imperative: Higher Expectations for Higher Education.* Racine, Wis.: Johnson Foundation, 1993.

ROBERT A. RHOADS is assistant professor in the Department of Educational Administration at Michigan State University. He is author of Community Service and Higher Learning: Explorations of the Caring Self *and* Freedom's Web: Student Activism in an Age of Cultural Diversity.

JEFFREY P. F. HOWARD is assistant director for academic service learning at the Center for Learning through Community Service, University of Michigan. He is founder and editor of the Michigan Journal of Community Service Learning.

This chapter discusses the elements of academic service learning and why this pedagogy is important for contemporary higher education.

Academic Service Learning: Its Meaning and Relevance

Kathleen Maas Weigert

For the new millennium, the critique of American culture seems to take on urgency in our public and private conversations. Whether in speeches of political leaders, in commentaries of public opinion analysts, or in conversations around the family table, we worry together about who we are as a nation, what is happening to us, and what needs to be done to ensure that in the twenty-first century we have greater vision, energy, and unity than we now have. What will our citizens be like? How will we define the common good? How will we respond to global challenges?

One specific concern is that the voices affirming the individualism strand of our tradition seem to be muffling those affirming the community strand (Bellah and others, 1985). A second and related issue is that the all-pervasive metaphor of the individual as a *consumer* crowds out such metaphors as *citizen* or *neighbor,* which capture and celebrate our interrelationships (Harwood Group, 1996). Finally, there is the charge that we are losing (or have lost) our shared family values and neighborhood ties; we seem to be more distant from others and more frazzled in our attempts to balance the varying demands of private and public life.

Part of this cultural critique focuses on higher education's role in society (Parks Daloz, Keen, Keen, and Daloz Parks, 1996). How are institutions of higher learning preparing students for active roles in public life? What "good" does college and university research provide for society? What is the responsibility of these institutions to the larger society, and are they fulfilling it?

In this context, attention to service learning takes on vital importance. Proponents of service learning contend that the cultural critique cited above must, first of all, be taken seriously; second, that service learning must provide

NEW DIRECTIONS FOR TEACHING AND LEARNING, no. 73, Spring 1998 © Jossey-Bass Publishers a positive though partial response to that cultural critique; and, third, that this pedagogy can offer potential advantages to all members—communities, students, faculty, colleges, and universities—through the work of forming new, challenging partnerships aimed at advancing knowledge and helping to remedy the deficiencies in our common life. The pedagogy is not risk-free, as proponents hasten to add, but it is precisely because the stakes are so high that the risk is worth taking.

This chapter has three purposes: to clarify what academic service learning entails; to identify some of the crucial debates in the field; and to invite faculty and administrators who are not yet familiar with it to consider its implementation. I first highlight some elements of contemporary higher education that serve as background for the growth and relevance of academic service learning, and then turn to a detailed examination of it.

Purposes of Higher Education Institutions

Institutions of higher education have multiple purposes. As articulated in the contemporary discourse, these purposes focus on teaching (and for many, the essential correlative, learning), research, and service. Part of the excitement of the current debate comes from the energy devoted to reconceptualizing the definitions and content of each of these purposes and, in the process, recognizing that they are not mutually exclusive. The late Ernest Boyer, perhaps more than any other individual, advocated expanding the definitions of the key terms and called for the academy to turn more attention and resources to the compelling needs of contemporary society (1990). In describing what he named the "New American College," for example, Boyer presented a vision of a new entity: "an institution that celebrates teaching and selectively supports research, while also taking special pride in its capacity to connect thought to action, theory to practice" (Boyer, 1994).

Each of the 3400 institutions of higher learning in this country addresses teaching, research, and service in its own way. One manifestation of uniqueness is found in the mission statement in which each institution spells out the key elements of its identity, goals, and aspirations. One often finds a section in the mission statement on how the institution conceives of its relationship to the local and larger community. Mission statements, important in themselves, only become real in the students, faculty, staff, and administrators who comprise the institution (see Chapter Nine).

Though we have national data on the professoriate (Magner, 1996) and incoming students (Astin, Korn, and Sax, 1994; Loeb, 1994), each institution nevertheless must undertake its own studies as well. What do the faculty and students think are the goals of this institution? What resources are available to meet those goals? What is valued and rewarded? Raising these questions opens a host of stimulating conversations, including the essential ones about what *teaching* means, what is important to teach, and how we know whether *learning* is taking place. Contemporary educators have contributed much to this debate with vibrant images and concepts: Citizenship Schools (Horton and

Freire, 1990), the banking and problem-posing models of education (Freire, 1993), education as a spiritual journey (Palmer, 1993), and education as the practice of freedom ("teaching to transgress") (hooks, 1994). It is into this conversation that practitioners of service learning enter.

Academic Service Learning in Higher Education

Service learning traces its roots to several important forces (Jacoby, 1996). One is certainly the decades-long work of organizations such as the National Society for Experiential Education and the Council for Adult and Experiential Learning, among others. In addition, several key events in the last decade have spurred the development of service learning. College students formed COOL (Campus Outreach Opportunity League) in 1984 with the mission to educate and empower students to strengthen the nation through service. In 1985 college and university presidents formed Campus Compact, an organization to expand opportunities for public and community service in higher education and to advocate the importance of civic responsibility in students' learning. In 1989 a small advisory group gathered at Wingspread and created "Principles of Good Practice for Combining Service and Learning" (Honnet and Poulsen, 1989). In 1994 The Invisible College was created as a gathering place for faculty interested in the integration of service and learning in higher education.

Elements of Academic Service Learning

Not surprisingly, definitions of service learning vary (see, for example, Honnet and Poulsen, 1989; Howard, 1993; Jacoby and Associates, 1996; Kendall and Associates, 1986; Rhoads, 1997). I suggest that at least six key elements, taken together, help differentiate service learning from voluntarism, community service, and other forms of experiential education (Kendall, 1990). Three of the elements focus more on the community side of the equation; the other three focus more on the campus side. On the community side: the student provides some meaningful service (work), that meets a need or goal, that is defined by a community (or some of its members). On the campus side: the service provided by the student flows from and into course objectives, is integrated into the course by means of assignments that require some form of reflection on the service in light of course objectives, and the assignment is assessed and evaluated accordingly.

To talk about service learning we must begin the conversation with a look at what is meant by *service*. *The Oxford English Dictionary* offers 38 definitions, among which we find a subset that focuses on help, benefit, and advantage, such as "conduct tending to the welfare or advantage of another" and "supply of the needs of persons." This seems to be what most practitioners have in mind at the most general level. Yet service is a marvelously complex and contested term. Let me highlight three issues to consider. First, what kind of attitudes do the provider of service and the recipient of the service bring to the experience?

If, for example, the student in a service learning course approaches the community with a "Messiah-complex," what are the chances that student and community will have a fruitful experience? Second, must the service be voluntary to be authentic? If, for example, a faculty requires service as part of the course, does this eviscerate the service? Third, is enhancement of citizenship intrinsic to all service learning courses, or is it the backdrop of much of service learning but not necessarily an essential goal of it?

In part because of these important questions, some prefer to talk about *community-based learning* or *community learning* rather than *service learning* (see Seidel and Zlotkowski, 1993). Community-based learning offers a conceptual space needed for developing more reciprocal relationships among the partners. With this term, for example, faculty and students can explicitly affirm that there are many sites of learning, including but not limited to the classroom. Students come to understand that they have an opportunity to gain new knowledge and insight through the service they provide in a community setting. Community representatives, as well as adult recipients of the service, can see themselves more as partners or co-teachers with the classroom teacher.

Let us examine each of the six elements of the definition, starting with the community side.

The student provides meaningful service. Some fear that the word *service* carries with it some negative messages (McKnight, 1989). An option is to use the word *work* as the descriptor of what students offer to the community. Whether the term *service* or *work* is preferred, a key concern is the adjective *meaningful*. It involves the notion of a significant amount of time dedicated to the service (although the amount is not universally agreed upon by all practitioners). It speaks to the issue of being useful or helpful, implying that the service makes a contribution, however small. In this context, preparation of students takes on a broader significance. If students are to work, for example, in an ethnic community or with a socioeconomic group different from their own, what preparation must they have before offering service to members of that community? Finally, in terms of defining what is meaningful, it is the community group making the request that is principally involved in that defining.

The service that students provide meets a need or goal of some kind. In other words, the service is not "make work." The service must be related somehow to a real need.

Members of a community define the need. Community is another one of the contested terms; it is rich in history and meaning. However it is conceived, it is certainly true that many people may define needs, including the faculty, who generally know what kinds of skills, attitudes, and preparation the students have. First-year, eighteen-year-old students in a liberal arts college, for example, will probably have abilities and skills different from those of senior-year, nontraditional-aged accounting students. In the conversation about what the community is seeking, needs or goals can be identified that might not otherwise have been recognized; in this interchange, the partners may uncover potential benefits they had not imagined.

Now let us turn to the elements on the campus side of the equation:

The service provided by the students flows from course objectives. Although some faculty design their courses with particular objectives in mind, for others the objectives remain at a fairly high level of abstraction. A first step is to be quite specific about course objectives and how various assignments address the objectives (Kendall and Associates, 1986). The faculty member can begin to think about alternative ways of meeting those objectives and how service in the community can be both feasible and appropriate to meet some course objective. A caution is in order: faculty should never dream up a service assignment that has nothing to do with the objectives of the course. Introductory course objectives will of necessity be different from those of a more advanced course; the faculty best knows for whom and for what the course is designed. The reader can find exciting examples of courses that incorporate service in a variety of sources (see Howard, 1993; Jackson, 1994; Kendall, 1990; Kupiec, 1993).

Service is integrated into the course by means of an assignment (or assignments) that requires some form of reflection on the service in light of course objectives. Having students in a community providing service is necessary but not sufficient for academic service learning to occur. There must be structured opportunities for the students to reflect on that service in light of course goals (Troppe, 1995). Faculty can employ a range of vehicles, from journals and other kinds of writing assignments to classroom discussions and oral presentations (Kendall, 1990; Kupiec, 1993; Troppe, 1995). In short, through the various assignments, service becomes an integral part of the academic work of the course.

Assignments rooted in the service must be assessed and evaluated accordingly. The standard refrain is this: We are grading the learning, not the service (Howard, 1993; Troppe, 1995). A simple analog is a reading assignment in, for example, a history course: We do not grade students on their reading, we grade them on their ability to demonstrate what they have learned from that reading. In parallel fashion, we must grade students' demonstrations of learning that come from the service assignment.

The community has a role in assessment. In employing service learning we are undertaking a partnership; all partners need to have some voice in the various aspects of the relationship. When it comes to assessing, faculty can invite input about the learning of each student from the community co-teacher through, for example, meetings or phone conversations or by asking the co-teacher to fill out an evaluation form that is then incorporated into the final assessment.

Some Critical Issues

In thinking about whether to incorporate service into a course or curricular program, faculty and administrators must address six other key issues in addition to those cited above.

Must a faculty member do service at the same time the students do? On the one hand, just as faculty read all the assigned texts for the course, should not faculty also do the assignment of service? In addition, since service in the community has potentially serious interpersonal consequences, does it not behoove faculty to have the experience of service to better understand and prepare students for the service? On the other hand is the practical issue of whether, in any particular semester or quarter, the faculty member has the necessary time to undertake the service. It may suffice that the faculty member has done the service at some point in time, not necessarily in the particular semester or quarter it is assigned for the students.

Should all students in a course, not just some, participate in service? Those in favor of the participation of all students argue, philosophically, that by having alternative assignments the faculty denies students a universal experience that is essential to the purposes of the course; pragmatically, they argue that it may be too difficult to have uniform grading standards across disparate assignments. Philosophically, those opposed contend that alternatives add richness to the class experience if the alternatives are shared with all students in some way; pragmatically, they contend that not all students can undertake a community-based assignment in a given semester or quarter for a variety of reasons, or that a community cannot absorb large numbers of students in supervised settings.

Are all placements equally legitimate for academic service learning? Some faculty and administrators judge that it is appropriate to place students only in *direct service* settings as opposed to *social action/social change* situations. They worry that the latter are more "political." Others maintain that all service learning placements are political in some way just as all have embedded in them a model of social change (Morton, 1995; see also Chapters Four and Five).

How can faculty get started? Clearly, if there is an office or a person hired to make links with the community, handle issues of transportation, deal with on-site supervision or monitoring, address legal concerns, and develop a number of placement sites, the work of faculty is greatly facilitated. Without such an infrastructure, faculty can still begin by locating a potential partner such as an agency in the local community. As the relationship develops, the partners can explore the opportunities for and obstacles to course linkages.

How are "failures" on a service learning assignment handled? One issue focuses on a student cheating (for example, claiming to have worked so many hours, which are written about for the assignment, when in fact the service was not done). The faculty or campus policies for handling cheating would come into play here as they do for any assignment. A related issue deals with the quality of the student's service. If the service is poorly rendered, what can be done? Did the student's service harm any recipients or damage any relationships? What is the community partner's perspective on the situation?

How does academic service learning relate to faculty reward structures? Will the faculty be penalized or rewarded for undertaking academic service learning? The National Project on Institutional Priorities and Faculty Rewards, coordinated at Syracuse University, is examining this pivotal concern. The Project operates on two key premises: "that redefining scholarship will expand the range of activities considered to be appropriate work for faculty members" and "that having disciplinary societies set out a full range of activities upon which tenure and promotion decisions can be based will help change the priorities for faculty members" (Diamond, 1994, p. B1).

Rewards of Academic Service Learning

Given the formidable challenges presented by service learning, why should faculty and administrators take on the hard work of incorporating service learning into their courses or institution? First, there is the joy that academic service learning provides. It can contribute to the renewal of the love of teaching that draws so many into higher education in the first place. Many faculty wanted, and still want, to have teaching and learning make a difference—for students, for themselves, and ultimately, for the world. Service learning not only makes that desire real again but also offers a way of effecting it. Second, because service learning crosses so many boundaries, it offers new opportunities to think more consciously and more creatively about relationships, including those of faculty and student, disciplinary and interdisciplinary or multidisciplinary knowledge, campus and community. Third, because service learning is an evolving field, those who enter it have the opportunity to contribute to its development. Fourth, because service learning calls for a link between what goes on in the classroom and what goes on in a community, it offers a vehicle to faculty, students, and community partners for thinking and responding in new, collaborative ways to the critical issues that confront our local and global worlds.

In short, academic service learning offers one avenue for rethinking and re-imagining the whats, whys, and for whoms of higher education in the context of contemporary criticisms.

References

Astin, A. W., Korn, W. A., and Sax, L. J. *The American Freshman: National Norms for Fall 1994.* Los Angeles: Higher Education Research Institute, University of California, 1994.

Bellah, R. N., Madsen, R., Sullivan, W. M., Swidler, A., and Tipton, S. M. *Habits of the Heart: Individualism and Commitment in American Life.* New York: HarperCollins, 1985.

Boyer, E. *Scholarship Reconsidered: Priorities of the Professoriate.* Princeton, N.J.: Carnegie Foundation for the Advancement of Teaching, 1990.

Boyer, E. "Creating the New American College." *Chronicle of Higher Education,* March 9, 1994, p. A48.

Diamond, R. M. "The Tough Task of Reforming the Faculty-Rewards System." *Chronicle of Higher Education,* May 11, 1994, pp. B1–B3.

Freire, P. *Pedagogy of the Oppressed.* (New revised 20th anniversary ed.) New York: Continuum, 1993. (Originally published 1970.)

Harwood Group. "Yearning for Balance." *YES! A Journal of Positive Futures,* 1996, no. 1B, 16–20.

Honnet, E. P., and Poulsen, S. J. *Principles of Good Practice for Combining Service and Learning.* Wingspread Special Report. Racine, Wis.: The Johnson Foundation, 1989.

hooks, b. *Teaching to Transgress: Education as the Practice of Freedom.* New York: Routledge, 1994.

Horton, M., and Freire, P. *We Make the Road by Walking: Conversations on Education and Social Change.* Philadelphia: Temple University Press, 1990.

Howard, J. (ed.). *Praxis I: A Faculty Casebook on Community Service Learning.* Ann Arbor, Mich.: OCSL Press, 1993.

Jackson, K. (ed.). *Redesigning Curricula: Models of Service Learning Syllabi.* Providence, R.I.: Campus Compact, 1994.

Jacoby, B. "Service-Learning in Today's Higher Education." In B. Jacoby and Associates, *Service-Learning in Higher Education: Concepts and Practices.* San Francisco: Jossey-Bass, 1996.

Kendall, J. C. (ed.). *Combining Service and Learning: A Resource Book for Community and Public Service.* Vol. 1. Raleigh, N.C.: National Society for Experiential Education, 1990.

Kendall, J., and Associates. *Strengthening Experiential Education Within Your Institution.* Raleigh, N.C.: National Society for Internships and Experiential Education, 1986.

Kupiec, T. Y. (ed.). *Rethinking Tradition: Integrating Service with Academic Study on College Campuses.* Providence, R.I.: Campus Compact, 1993.

Loeb, P. R. *Generations at the Crossroads: Apathy and Action on the American Campus.* New Brunswick, N.J.: Rutgers University Press, 1994.

Magner, D. K. "Fewer Professors Believe Western Culture Should Be the Cornerstone of the College Curriculum." *Chronicle of Higher Education,* Sept. 13, 1996, pp. A12–A13.

McKnight, J. "Why 'Servanthood' Is Bad." *The Other Side,* 1989, 25 (1), 38–40.

Morton, K. "The Irony of Service: Charity, Project and Social Change in Service Learning." *Michigan Journal of Community Service Learning,* 1995, 2 (1), 19–32.

Palmer, P. J. *To Know As We Are Known: Education As a Spiritual Journey.* San Francisco: HarperCollins, 1993. (Originally published 1983.)

Parks Daloz, L. S., Keen, C. H., Keen, J. P., and Daloz Parks, S. "Lives of Commitment: Higher Education in the Life of the New Commons." *Change,* May/June 1996, pp. 11–15.

Rhoads, R. A. *Community Service and Higher Learning: Explorations of the Caring Self.* Albany: State University of New York Press, 1997.

Seidel, R., and Zlotkowski, E. "Common Ground: From Service-Learning to Community-Learning." *Experiential Education,* 1993, 18 (3), 10, 15.

Troppe, M. (ed.). *Connecting Cognition and Action: Evaluation of Student Performance in Service-Learning Courses.* Providence, R.I.: Campus Compact, 1995.

KATHLEEN MAAS WEIGERT is associate director for academic affairs and research, Center for Social Concerns; concurrent associate professor, American studies; and fellow, The Joan B. Kroc Institute for International Peace Studies, at the University of Notre Dame.

The theoretical bases of academic service learning are examined, with particular attention to John Dewey's contributions. The service learning movement is conceptualized as part of an ongoing—and still unsuccessful—effort to "de-Platonize" and democratize American higher education in particular and American schooling in general.

De-Platonizing and Democratizing Education as the Bases of Service Learning

Ira Harkavy, Lee Benson

Academic service learning is a pedagogy derived from a theory of democratic education and schooling developed by John Dewey to replace Plato's aristocratic theory of education and society. At minimum, Dewey's theory asserts four propositions:

1. "Reflective thought is an active response to the challenge of the environment" (Smith, 1983, p. 124).
2. Individuals learn best when they participate "in the formation of the purposes that govern their activities" (Nicholls and Hazzard, 1995, p. 114).
3. All individuals can contribute to knowledge.
4. The fundamental purpose of knowledge is to improve human welfare.

Although Dewey did not originate all four propositions, he developed a theory of instrumental intelligence and democratic education that significantly advanced and integrated them. It can fairly be said: In the beginning there was Dewey. Dewey's work, however, is not the sole source of current practice and theory. Important predecessors, related but generally independent thinkers and doers, and latter-day Deweyans have also contributed to academic service learning.

To overestimate the impact of Platonic thought on Western philosophy would be nearly impossible. A proposition asserted by A. N. Whitehead succinctly captures Plato's preeminent influence: "The whole later development of Western philosophy can be regarded as a series of extended footnotes to Plato" (Margetson, 1994, p. 7). Uncompromisingly aristocratic and antidemocratic, Platonic thought has had perhaps its greatest (and most pernicious) impact on Western education.

For Plato, learning occurred through contemplative thought, not through action and reflection. Dividing the world into ideal and material universes, Plato viewed knowledge as deriving from the ideal, spiritual universe of permanent and fixed ideas. He conceptualized the material world of objects and actions as merely "a shadowy, fleeting world" of imperfect imitations (Butts, 1955, p. 46).

Just as ideas were fixed and permanent for Plato, so too were society's classes and their characteristics. Knowledge could not be attained by the vast mass of people who did society's basic work; and the warrior class could attain only imperfect knowledge since its members' thoughts were tied to the material world. True knowledge was the province of the ruling class, those few men capable of going beyond the sensate and material world to the eternal world of ideas. Plato designed an educational system that would sort people into one of the three classes, with major attention and resources provided to those destined to become philosopher-kings. Fixed truths, rigid classes, and advanced education for the few are concepts that fit well with the antidemocratic, aristocratic form of society that Plato advocated to overcome the "evils" of Athenian "democracy."

Academic service learning can be conceptualized as an attempt to release the vice-like grip that the dead hand of Plato has had, and continues to have, on American schooling and education. Although anti-Platonic precursors of service learning can be found as early as Cicero in the first century B.C., Francis Bacon provides a more useful starting point for our discussion (Sullivan, 1996, pp. 17–18).

Francis Bacon and the Production and Use of Knowledge

Bacon's work contributed powerfully to the seventeenth-century Scientific Revolution and the idea of progress it helped to inspire. He promoted the idea that replacing ancient scholastic science with a modern experimental science of inquiry and effective organization for collaborative work would greatly advance knowledge for "the relief of man's estate," that is, continual human betterment (as quoted in Benson, 1978, p. 429).

Dewey praised Bacon as "the great forerunner of the spirit of modern life," the "prophet of new tendencies," and the "real founder of modern thought" (1948 [1920], pp. 28–32). In Dewey's view, Bacon's far-reaching proposition that knowledge is power provided the pragmatic criterion needed to test, assess, and demonstrate the relative effectiveness of traditional (Platonic) and modern modes of inquiry.

For Bacon, progress is dependent upon both the production and use of knowledge. If production were isolated or separated from use, the results would not be beneficial. For knowledge to function as power for good, effective organization must dynamically and systematically plan for the integrated production and use of knowledge. Undertaken for the wrong (amoral or immoral) reasons, the production of new knowledge, moreover, could have dreadful consequences. Knowledge, Bacon contended, should be pursued "for the benefit and the use of life," not "for pleasure of the mind, or for contention, or for superiority to others, or for profit, or fame, or power, or any of those inferior things" (as quoted in Farrington, 1949, pp. 88–89).

Bacon's challenge to Platonic thought included a rejection of the ancient Greek aristocratic false dualism between "superior" pure theory and "inferior" applied practice. As Benjamin Farrington has emphasized: "Bacon insisted again and again on the virtual identity of scientific truth and practical utility. What is most useful in practice is most correct in theory. . . . The improvement of man's mind and the improvement of his lot are one and the same thing"(1949, p. 98).

Bacon's promotion of progress as the standard to judge inquiry, his emphasis on both the production and humane use of knowledge, and his linkage of practice and theory all constituted "a sustained attack on traditional philosophy" (Box, 1989, pp. 2–3). That attack also included a participatory democratic conception of the organization and conduct of scientific inquiry, one radically at odds with Plato's elitist, antidemocratic theory and plan. For Bacon, (almost) all human beings continuously have to try to solve problems affecting their well-being. If the mass of human beings were educated, therefore, to engage in their real-world problem-solving in the spirit of, and with the methods of, modern experimental scientific inquiry, *and if scientific inquiry were appropriately organized,* then the results of their daily problem-solving could contribute measurably to "new facts and new truths." Or, as Ian Box emphasized in his *Social Thought of Francis Bacon*: "The project did not depend on the unique genius of a Plato or an Aristotle, but was open to every man's industry. *Everyone could contribute to the progressive interpretation of nature* [emphasis added]" (1989, pp. 2–3; Benson and Harkavy, 1994, pp. 68–69).

Bacon strongly argued that the effective organization of inquiry was necessary if knowledge was to be produced and used for humane ends. In his Utopian fable, *The New Atlantis* (1627), Bacon sketched a comprehensive organizational system for the increasingly progressive, integrated production and use of knowledge. Bacon's vision of the appropriate organization of research was so radical and comprehensive that, even today, it remains far from realization. It would be an eighteenth-century disciple of Bacon, Benjamin Franklin, who would propose creating a college devoted to public service. In so doing, Franklin identified an institutional vehicle capable of putting Bacon's noble vision into practice.

Franklin's Contribution: Service and the Reformation of Higher Education

Contemptuous of scholasticism and devoted to Bacon's modern experimental philosophy, Franklin acted on the proposition that effective organization was mandatory if knowledge was to function as power and help achieve the "relief of man's estate." In 1743, Franklin proposed the establishment of two Bacon-inspired organizational innovations in Philadelphia. One eventually became the present-day American Philosophical Society for Promoting Useful Knowledge, the other, the University of Pennsylvania.

Franklin's ideas focused on a course of study that would include English grammar and composition, public speaking, history, geography, mathematics and accounting, natural history, scientific experiments, and ethics. Most centrally, the curriculum would be infused with public service; it would be an education for citizenship and service. The college would be an institution of higher education to train an elite, teach them useful knowledge, and develop their capacity to learn and to produce useful knowledge. Above all, however, it would inculcate the Baconian ideal of acquiring and pursuing knowledge for the "benefit and use of life."

Franklin's ideas were never adopted at the University of Pennsylvania. To some extent, however, during the 1890s, Seth Low, president of Columbia University, put them into practice by consciously intertwining Columbia with New York City; and John Dewey at the University of Chicago developed a theory of instrumental intelligence that served as the philosophical basis of academic service learning.

Seth Low's Columbia as a Cosmopolitan, Democratic, Civic University

In the late nineteenth and early twentieth centuries, Columbia, like other leading urban universities—for example, Johns Hopkins, the University of Pennsylvania, and the University of Chicago—seized the opportunity to advance knowledge, teaching, and learning by working to improve the quality of life in American cities experiencing the traumatic effects of industrialization, immigration, and large-scale urbanization (Benson and Harkavy, 1997a; Harkavy, 1996). Seth Low, Columbia's president from 1890 through 1901, is notable for his enthusiastic embrace of New York City as the source of the university's greatness. He not only brought "the College into closer touch with the community," but he also significantly improved Columbia by successfully encouraging faculty and students to focus their intellectual work on helping New York solve its problems (Low as quoted in Kurland, 1971, p. 53).

A mediocre institution in the 1870s and 1880s, Columbia was widely viewed as a snobbish school for rich young men. In his inaugural address, Low echoed Bacon's and Franklin's proposition that the purpose of scholarship is service for the betterment of humanity, and actually went beyond by posing and answering the question, "Knowledge for what?" He called on students and professors to become engaged directly with the city and its communities and people. Engagement with, and study and action in New York City, according to Low, would produce liberally educated and moral students, as well as "worldly," "unpedantic" professors inspired and equipped to contribute profoundly to the advancement of knowledge (Cary, 1897, pp. 10, 40–41).

No other university president had so clearly articulated a morally inspired, instrumental, active approach to research, teaching, and learning. In effect, repudiating Plato's notion of the groves of academe with its physical and intellectual separation of town and gown, Low linked town and gown, identifying a mutually beneficial, interactive relationship between Columbia and the city as crucial to intellectual and institutional advancement. Low even went so far as to invoke Bacon's standard of progress as the test of inquiry and research. In Low's case, the specific test was Columbia's ability "to influence the life of New York" (Bender, 1987, p. 284). That influence would not result, moreover, from the authoritative, elitist, university-dominated approach advocated by many of the most "progressive" Progressive-era academics. To the contrary, Low's approach was decidedly democratic in dealing with the city and its people. Learning would be, he emphasized, reciprocal and interactive: "Workingmen of America . . . [should know] that at Columbia College . . . the disposition exists to teach the truth . . . without fear or favor, and we *ask their aid to enable us to see the truth as it appears to them* [emphasis added]" (Bender, 1987, p. 283).

Low's extraordinary contributions to Columbia and to the practice and theory of instrumental education have largely been forgotten. His vision of a cosmopolitan, democratic, civic university was significantly ahead of its time. Moreover, the brevity of his tenure, the forty-three year imperious reign of his successor (Nicholas Murray Butler), and the dominance of Plato's aristocratic, scholastic, "liberal" educational theory in American colleges and universities also account for Low's limited impact. In recent years, increasing critiques of the performance of internally directed, solipsistic ivory towers and the concomitant call for higher education to help solve the serious problems confronting American society have led to a nascent interest in Columbia during the Low years. These same factors have contributed to the "Dewey revival" affecting scholarship across many disciplines, simultaneously shaping educational practice through academic service learning and related pedagogies.

Dewey's Theory of Instrumental Intelligence and Democratic Instrumental Education

Though he never wrote directly about service learning, Dewey's contributions to academic service learning are so varied and rich that it is a subject worthy of many books. Summarized succinctly, Dewey developed a theory of instrumental intelligence and democratic instrumental education that provides the underpinnings for the growing democratic "crusade" against Plato's aristocratic, idealist, contemplative philosophy. Dewey explicitly conceptualized his work as a critique of the philosophy and methods of the "Old Education," when "learning was a class matter," and "a high priesthood of learning . . . guarded the truth and . . . doled it out to the masses under severe restrictions" (1990 [1900], pp. 24–26). Existing American schools, as Dewey viewed them, were largely derived from and dominated by those antiquated, highly dysfunctional, aristocratic, monastic models. In 1899 he wrote: "The ideals of this period are still largely in control, even where the outward methods and studies have changed . . . our present education . . . is . . . dominated almost entirely by the medieval conception of learning" (1990 [1900], pp. 24–26).

Dewey's critique of the "almost entirely . . . medieval" American public school system had two interrelated dimensions: the system was radically dysfunctional for industrially advanced American society; it was radically antithetical to American democratic ideals. For Dewey, if there were no democratic education and schooling system, there could be no genuinely democratic society. An aristocratic, idealist, scholastic Greek "liberal" theory of education was appropriate for and supportive of an aristocratic social order—but highly inappropriate for a democratic social order. Dewey further argued that traditional schooling created "passivity of attitude," with devastating effects on a child's ability to learn, to develop his or her own talents, and to become an active, participatory citizen (1990 [1900], pp. 31–34).

Dewey's theory of democratic or "New Education" emphasized that students should be able to help shape their own learning, help form their curriculum, and reflect on its value. Democracy and learning, for Dewey, would both be advanced if human beings were engaged in active real-world problem-solving that entailed ongoing "intelligent judgment and action" (as quoted in Westbrook, 1991, p. xv). In 1938, Dewey emphatically asserted that "there is . . . no point in the philosophy of progressive education which is sounder than the emphasis upon the importance of the participation of the learner in the formation of the purpose which directs his activities in the learning process" (Nicholls and Hazzard, 1995, p. 115).

At the heart of Dewey's approach is a theory of instrumental intelligence that rejects Platonic dualisms that counterpose practice and theory, material and ideal, and so on. To quote Donald Schön: "In the domain of practice, we see what John Dewey called *inquiry*: thought intertwined with action—which proceeds from doubt to the resolution of doubt, to the generation of new doubt. For Dewey, doubt lies not in the mind but in the situation. Inquiry begins with situations that are problematic—that are confusing, uncertain, or conflicted, and block the free flow of action" (1995, p. 31). Put another way, genuine learning, according to Dewey, only occurs when human beings focus their attention, energies, and abilities on solving genuine dilemmas and perplexities—and when they reflect on their experience and, therefore, increase their capacity for future intelligent thought and action. Intelligence does not develop simply as a result of action and experience, it develops as a result of *reflective* action and experience (Benson and Harkavy, 1997b).

If we use the Baconian test of progress both in society and scholarship, we find that Dewey's work has had a mixed result. Dewey's Laboratory School at the University of Chicago, the primary means for putting his ideas into practice, certainly did not revolutionize the American public school system. It did, however, serve as the most important vehicle for disseminating the ideas of the

University of Chicago's philosophy department. The work of the department produced an extraordinary achievement—the development of Chicago Pragmatism. Hailed by William James as so "wonderful . . . [that] it deserves the title of a new system of philosophy," the Chicago School emerged from the action-oriented engagement of Dewey and his colleagues in the real-world problems of the city in which they lived and worked (Rucker, 1969, pp. 3–4). Indeed, from the University of Chicago's founding in 1892 through and beyond Dewey's departure to Columbia in 1904, the city's reform movement was closely tied to the university. Dewey, James H. Tufts, and George Herbert Mead, for example, all played leading roles in the efforts to improve education and politics in the city (Shils, 1988). According to a leading authority on the Chicago Pragmatists, moreover, these "practical endeavors were encouraged as fitting for a university providing a broad field of testing ideas and theories" (Rucker, 1969, p. 9).

There are obviously striking parallels between Low's Columbia and Dewey's Chicago. The city, with its problems and rich opportunities, served in both cases as the focal point and wellspring of action, learning, and scholarship. In both cases, a real-world, action-oriented academic strategy produced significant institutional and intellectual advances.

In 1927, many years after he had left Chicago, Dewey unequivocally identified the existence of "neighborly community" as indispensable for a well-functioning democratic society: "There is no substitute for the vitality and depth of close and direct intercourse and attachment. . . . Democracy begins at home, and its home is the neighborly community." In that same book, *The Public and Its Problems*, he also noted that creating a genuinely democratic community is "in the first instance an intellectual problem" (pp. 213, 147).

Dewey in effect identified the central societal problem (and therefore central intellectual problem) of human societies in the twentieth century to be the actual construction of what we have termed "cosmopolitan neighborly communities." The discussion of community in *The Public and Its Problems*, along with the extraordinary success achieved by "progressive academics" at Chicago and Columbia (and other urban universities) at the turn of the twentieth century, provide a powerful case for a community problem-solving focus for college and university research, teaching, and service. Thus, strategic, academically based community scholarship and service—a particularly significant variant of academically based service learning—can also be traced to Dewey's seminal activities and writings. Strategic, academically based community scholarship and service involves the integration of research, teaching, and service, and aims to bring about structural community improvement (for example, effective public schools, neighborhood economic development, strong community organizations) rather than simply to alleviate individual misery (for example, feeding the hungry, sheltering the homeless, tutoring the "slow learner"). It has as its primary goal contributing to the well-being of people in the community, both in the here and now and in the future (Harkavy, 1996; Lawson, 1997).

Notwithstanding Dewey's far-reaching contribution to current practice and theory, he never systematically explored how to get from a Plato-inspired, aristocratic, idealist schooling system to a system of democratic instrumental education. Dewey's writings, however, do contain a wide variety of fruitful general ideas, insights, and propositions that, when appropriately applied in practice, can be used to put the "New Education" into practice. Dewey's work, for example, adumbrates the method of participatory action research, which has played an increasingly significant role in academic service learning. It was the eminent social psychologist, Kurt Lewin, however, who labeled and operationalized the approach.

Kurt Lewin and Action Research

A true heir of Bacon, Lewin held that "research that produces nothing but books will not suffice" (as quoted in Turner, 1986, p. 201). His most well-known aphorism, "there is nothing so practical as a good theory," is a clear rejection of Platonic dualism and a call for connecting scholarship and the real world (Lewin, 1964, p. 169; Marrow, 1969). Lewin worked toward the development of "actionable theory"; that is, theory constructed, applied, tested, and revised in "particular situations of practice" (Schön, 1995, p. 31).

Lewin's commitment to action research in service to a better society is evident in the connection he made between the Research Center for Group Dynamics at the Massachusetts Institute of Technology, which he created and directed, and the American Jewish Congress's Commission on Community Interrelations (CCI). The CCI conducted action research on community affairs, focusing on minority problems, ethnocultural conflict, and discriminatory attitudes and behavior. Lewin's work with the Commission strongly resonates with Dewey's theory of instrumental intelligence while providing a research strategy that embeds and integrates both action and reflection (Harkavy and Puckett, 1997).

In effect, Lewin developed a method to help extend and realize Dewey's philosophy and theories. David Kolb's work on experiential education (1984) and Donald Schön's study of the professions and the "reflective practitioner" (1983) both discuss the similarities between the work of Dewey and Lewin. Indeed, Kolb and Schön are two important contributors to the practice of academic service learning. Their writings, as well as those of Ernest Boyer (1994), have helped in different ways to bring the ideas of Bacon, Franklin, Low, Dewey, and Lewin into current discussion and use.

Conclusion

We conclude with Dewey's brilliant observation that "the true starting point of history is always some present situation with its problems" (1916, p. 251). The present situation informing this essay is the increasing development of academic service learning in colleges and universities haunted by the "living ghost" of

Plato—a living ghost that functions as an incubus on the body of the entire American system of schooling. The core problem embedded in that situation is: How can academic service learning, particularly academically based community scholarship and service, help overthrow the aristocratic Platonic theory of "liberal education" and institute a democratic Deweyan theory of "instrumental education?" The history sketched above aims to help service learners and practitioners/theorists better use and understand the work of their predecessors so that they (we) might speed the radical, long overdue, "de-Platonization" of American higher education in particular and American schooling in general.

"Overthrowing Plato and instituting Dewey" should constitute the categorical imperative—the revolutionary slogan—of the service learning movement in the twenty-first century.

References

Bacon, F. *The New Atlantis*. Kila, Mont.: Kessinger, 1992.

Bender, T. *The New York Intellect*. Baltimore: Johns Hopkins University Press, 1987.

Benson, L. "Changing Social Science to Change the World: Discussion Paper." *Social Science History*, 1978, 2, 427–441.

Benson, L., and Harkavy, I. "Progressing Beyond the Welfare State." *Universities and Community Schools*, 1991, 2 (1–2), 2–28.

Benson, L., and Harkavy, I. "Anthropology 210, Academically-Based Community Service, and the Advancement of Knowledge, Teaching and Learning: An Experiment in Progress." *Universities and Community Schools*, 1994, 4 (1–2), 66–69.

Benson, L., and Harkavy, I. "Introduction: Universities, Colleges, and Their Neighboring Communities." *Universities and Community Schools*, 1997a, 5 (1–2), 5–11.

Benson, L., and Harkavy, I. "School and Community in the Global Society." *Universities and Community Schools*, 1997b, 5 (1–2), 16–71.

Box, I. *The Social Thought of Francis Bacon*. Lewiston, N.Y.: Edwin Mellen Press, 1989.

Boyer, E. L. "Creating the New American College." *Chronicle of Higher Education*, March 9, 1994, p. A48.

Butts, R. F. *A Cultural History of Western Education*. New York: McGraw-Hill, 1955.

Cary, E. "Seth Low: A Character Sketch." *Review of Reviews*, 1897, no. 16, 33–42.

Dewey, J. *Democracy and Education*. New York: Macmillan, 1916.

Dewey, J. *The Public and Its Problems*. New York: Holt, 1927.

Dewey, J. *Reconstruction in Philosophy*. Boston: Beacon, 1948. (Originally published 1920.)

Dewey, J. *School and Society*. Chicago: University of Chicago Press, 1990. (Originally published 1900; rev. ed. 1915.)

Farrington, B. *Francis Bacon: Philosopher of Industrial Science*. New York: Henry Schuman, 1949.

Harkavy, I. "Back to the Future: From Service Learning to Strategic Academically-Based Community Service." *Metropolitan Universities*, 1996, 7 (1), 57–70.

Harkavy, I., and Puckett, J. "The Action Research Tradition in American Social Science." Unpublished manuscript, Center for Community Partnerships, University of Pennsylvania, 1997.

Kolb, D. A. *Experiential Learning*. Englewood Cliffs, N.J.: Prentice Hall, 1984.

Kurland, G. *Seth Low: The Reformer in an Urban and Industrial Age*. New York: Twayne, 1971.

Lawson, H. A. "Academically-Based Community Scholarship and a Collective Responsibility Model." Unpublished manuscript, PHS Department, Miami University, 1997.

Lewin, K. "Problems of Research in Social Psychology." In D. Cartwright (ed.), *Field Theory in Social Science*. New York: HarperCollins, 1964.

Margetson, D. "Current Educational Reform and the Significance of Problem-Based Learning." *Occasional Papers*, no. 1. [http://www.gu.edu.au/gwis/gihe/gihe_op/op1_margetson.html]. 1994.

Marrow, A. J. *The Practical Theorist.* New York: Basic Books, 1969.

Nicholls, J. G., and Hazzard, S. P. "Students as Collaborators in Curriculum Construction." In J. G. Nicholls and T. A. Thorkildsen (eds.), *Reasons for Learning.* New York: Teachers College Press, 1995.

Rucker, D. *The Chicago Pragmatists.* Minneapolis: University of Minnesota Press, 1969.

Schön, D. A. *The Reflective Practitioner.* New York: Basic Books, 1983.

Schön, D. A. "Knowing in Action: The New Scholarship Requires a New Epistemology." *Change,* Nov./Dec. 1995, pp. 27–34.

Shils, E. "The University, the City, and the World: Chicago and the University of Chicago." In T. Bender (ed.), *The University and the City.* New York: Oxford University Press, 1988.

Smith, J. E. *The Spirit of American Philosophy.* (Rev. ed.) Albany: State University of New York Press, 1983.

Sullivan, W. M. "The Public Intellectual As Transgressor?" *The Higher Education Exchange.* Dayton, Ohio: Kettering Foundation, 1996.

Turner, J., "Community Action Research in North Philadelphia." In E. Stivers and S. Wheelan (eds.), *The Lewin Legacy.* Berlin: Springer-Verlag, 1986.

Westbrook, R. B. *John Dewey and American Democracy.* Ithaca, N.Y.: Cornell University Press, 1991.

IRA HARKAVY is associate vice president and director of the Center for Community Partnerships at the University of Pennsylvania.

LEE BENSON is emeritus professor of history at the University of Pennsylvania. He and Ira Harkavy are executive editors of Universities and Community Schools.

Creating a service learning course raises substantive pedagogical challenges and dilemmas. This chapter discusses the counternormative nature of academic service learning and presents a pedagogical model to resolve these tensions.

Academic Service Learning: A Counternormative Pedagogy

Jeffrey P. F. Howard

Faculty interest in academic service learning has exploded over the last few years. Some see service learning as a way to prepare students for active citizenship. Others perceive it as a means to involve universities in socially responsible action. Still others find in it a panacea for the perceived shortcomings of the information-dissemination model that prevails in higher education.

These are solid reasons for becoming involved in academic service learning. But once the motivation for becoming involved has emerged, questions about implementation necessarily arise. Though the notion of adding community service to an academic course may not be difficult to conceptualize, the practice of integrating service and learning is anything but simple.

Contrary to some interpretations, academic service learning is not merely the addition of a community service option or requirement to an academic course. A clause on a syllabus that directs students to complete community service hours as a course requirement or in lieu of another course assignment does not constitute academic service learning. Rather than serving as a parallel or sidebar activity, the students' community service experiences in academic service learning function as a critical learning complement to the academic goals of the course.

In other words, academic service learning is not about the addition of service to learning, but rather the integration of service with learning. In this contrasting *synergistic* model, the students' community service experiences are compatible and integrated with the academic learning objectives of the course, in a manner similar to traditional course requirements. Here students' observations and experiences in the community setting are as pivotal to the students' academic learning as class lectures and library research. In this integrated

21

model, the service and the learning are reciprocally related; the service experiences inform and transform the academic learning, and the academic learning informs and transforms the service experience (Honnet and Poulsen, 1989).

Integrating service with academic learning, however, catalyzes a complexity to the teaching-learning process that is analogous to adding a newborn to a family. Just as the newborn is not merely the addition of one more member to the family, community service is not merely the addition of one more requirement to a course. As the newborn qualitatively changes the norms and relationships in the family constellation, so, too, community service qualitatively changes the norms and relationships in the teaching-learning process.

A Working Definition of Academic Service Learning

For the purposes of this volume, we are utilizing the working definition, "Academic service learning is a pedagogical model that intentionally integrates academic learning and relevant community service." There are four key components to this definition. First, academic service learning is a *pedagogical model*; first and foremost it is a teaching methodology, more than a values model, leadership development model, or a social responsibility model. Second, there is an *intentional* effort made to utilize the community-based learning on behalf of academic learning, and to utilize academic learning to inform the community service. This presupposes that academic service learning will not happen unless a concerted effort is made to harvest community-based learning and strategically bridge it with academic learning. Third, there is an *integration* of the two kinds of learning, experiential and academic; they work to strengthen one another. Finally, the community service experiences must be *relevant* to the academic course of study (Howard, 1993). Serving in a soup kitchen is relevant for a course on social issues but probably not for a course on civil engineering. All four components are necessary in the practice of academic service learning.

Challenges

From this definition, it is apparent that academic service learning creates a host of stimulating pedagogical challenges that are obviated in traditional pedagogy. For example, how can we strengthen student capacity to extract meaning from community experiences? How can we strengthen student capacity to utilize community-based learning on behalf of academic learning? How can we better enable students to apply their academic learning to their community service? These are challenges that those who consider academic service learning will face.

Many of the pedagogical challenges associated with academic service learning result from its counternormative nature. Academic service learning stands, in some significant ways, in contradistinction to traditional pedagogical principles. For example, broadening the learning environment beyond the instructor's purview is clearly contrary to standard pedagogical operating procedures. Involving students in experiential learning breaches traditional practice. Positioning students with the responsibility for discerning important from unimportant "data" in the community is contrary to traditional courses in which relevant knowledge is deciphered for the students by the instructor. The mix of traditional classroom-based theoretical learning and nontraditional community-based experiential learning clearly "raises the pedagogical bar."

The Traditional Pedagogical Model

At the risk of generalization and simplification, let us review some of the salient features of the prevailing information-dissemination model in higher education. The oft-cited advantage of this model, customarily manifested in the lecture, is that it is efficient in transmitting volumes of academic information and theory to large numbers of students. Through years of elementary and secondary school rehearsal and then higher education reinforcement, classroom roles, relationships, and norms in the traditional model have been powerfully internalized by all parties; before entering the very first meeting of a class, faculty and students alike know that faculty are the knowledge experts and direct the learning activities in the course, and that students begin with knowledge deficits and follow the prescribed learning activities. In this "banking model" (Freire, 1970), faculty are active, depositing and periodically withdrawing intellectual capital from students who are for the most part passive. The course follows a predetermined structure, learning stimuli are uniform for all students, and each class and each assignment follow a familiar routine. Even in courses in which there is a departure from the standard lecture, "discussion usually focuses on a pre-established set of inquiry questions or curricula" (Chesler, 1993, p. 31). In fact, control of the entire range of teaching and learning activity is within the faculty member's knowledge and experience purview and ascribed and perceived jurisdiction.

Furthermore, in the traditional teaching-learning model, learning is individualistic and privatized; students generally learn by themselves and for themselves. When students do contribute in class discussions, often it is for grade-enhancing reasons rather than to advance their peers' learning. Instructor-determined grades reflect individual achievement. The epistemology that undergirds traditional pedagogy is positivistic and in conflict with communal ways of learning (Palmer, 1990).

Incongruencies Between the Two Pedagogies

Academic service learning is incongruent with traditional pedagogy in a number of ways:

A conflict of goals. Service learning's goal of advancing students' sense of social responsibility or commitment to the broader good conflicts with the individualistic, self-orientation of the traditional classroom (Howard, 1993). Perhaps the most important way that academic service learning is inconsistent with traditional pedagogy, and even other forms of experiential learning, is in its insistence on advancing students' commitment to the greater good. "The competitive individualism of the classroom . . . reflects a pedagogy that stresses the individual as the prime agent of knowing" (Palmer, 1990, p. 111). In the traditional course, with its focus on the individual, an orientation toward others is necessarily discouraged. The dilemma here is that the nature of the traditional classroom encourages individual responsibility rather than social responsibility.

A conflict about valuable learning. In traditional courses, academic learning is valued, whereas in academic service learning, academic learning is valued *along with* community-based experiential learning. Academic learning is deductively oriented, whereas experiential learning is inductively oriented. The dilemma here is how these very different kinds and ways of learning not only can coexist but can even create a learning synergy for students.

A conflict about control. In traditional courses there is a high degree of structure and direction vis-à-vis learning; the faculty control what is important for students to learn. This contrasts with an invariably low degree of structure and direction vis-à-vis learning in the community (the exception may be professional practica, in which there is directed learning by a designated field placement supervisor). Therefore, in the community, students are more likely to be in charge of their learning. Even though they may be armed with a learning schema from the instructor, the dilemma is how to bring the level of learning structure and direction in the two learning contexts into greater congruence.

A conflict about active learning. A closely related issue is that student passivity contributes to the efficiency of the information-dissemination model, whereas in the community there is a premium on active learning. The high degree of structure and direction provided by the instructor in traditional pedagogy leads to a passive learning posture by students, but the low degree of structure and direction in communities in relation to learning requires that students assume an active learning posture. The dilemma here is how to bring the role of the learner in the classroom into greater congruence with the role of the learner in the community.

A conflict about contributions from students. The orientation toward efficient transmission of information in the traditional model precludes taking advantage of students' learning in the community. Student contributions in traditional pedagogy are discouraged because they compromise the efficiency goal. The dilemma here is how to make student learning that is harvested in the community not only welcome but utilized in the classroom.

A conflict about objectivity. Whereas objectivity is valued in the traditional classroom, in academic service learning a subjective engagement, emanating from the philosophy of pragmatism, is also valued (Liu, 1995). The dilemma here is how to integrate subjective and objective ways of knowing.

A New Model: The Synergistic Classroom

To resolve these tensions, drastic measures are needed. Nothing less than a reconceptualization of the teaching-learning process will do. We need a pedagogical model that

- Encourages social responsibility
- Values and integrates both academic and experiential learning
- Accommodates both high and low levels of structure and direction
- Embraces the active, participatory student
- Welcomes both subjective and objective ways of knowing.

For many years I have struggled with these dilemmas in a sociology service learning course here at the University of Michigan. I have struggled in my attempts to prompt student participation, to find a balance between more structure and less structure, to integrate learning from the community with learning from academic readings, and to encourage social responsibility in the classroom.

Over time I have come to realize that to create a classroom that is consistent with the goals and values of service learning, it is absolutely necessary to deprogram or desocialize students and instructors away from traditional classroom roles, relationships, and norms, and then resocialize them around a new set of classroom behaviors. To accomplish the desocialization and resocialization processes requires that the instructor and the students *travel together* on a journey to remake the classroom. Figure 3.1 depicts this journey.

Figure 3.1. Stages in Transforming the Classroom

	Passive	
Stage 1 Traditional classroom (*conform*)	Student	*Stage 2* Instructor desocialization/ resocialization (*renorm*)
Directive —————————————— Instructor	behavior	—————————————— Facilitative
Stage 3 Student desocialization/ resocialization (*storm*)	behavior	*Stage 4* Synergistic classroom (*perform*)
	Active	

In this matrix, four prototypical stages are identified in moving from a traditional classroom to a synergistic classroom that meets the five criteria enumerated above. The first stage, identified as the *conform* stage, depicts the traditional classroom model in which the instructor (represented on the horizontal axis) is directive and the students (represented on the vertical axis) are passive. To initiate the transformation process, identified in the model as the second stage, *renorm*, the instructor must begin to carry out her or his role in an intentionally counternormative way. For example, the instructor may ask students what was important in their readings and in their service experiences since the last class, and use their contributions to frame the class discussion. Actions such as this will implicitly communicate to the students that it will not be business as usual.

In this second stage, however, the students, whose schooling has been effective in internalizing a passive, individualistic role in the classroom, resist these change efforts and continue to be primarily passive. This might be manifested in a low participation rate when the instructor seeks contributions from the students. But as the instructor continues to be consistent in her or his new interpretation of the teacher role, and as the students continue to receive the message that their active participation around both academic and community-based learning is encouraged, we arrive at stage 3 in which the students, in fact, become more active and begin to take greater responsibility for the learning in the classroom.

This *storm* stage, ironically, often becomes problematic for the instructor, who, also schooled for many years to perceive instructors as authorities and students as receptacles, questions the quality of learning under way. As a result, in this third stage the instructor regresses and retreats to a more directive posture. But over time, the instructor comes to realize that the students are genuinely learning, and returns to a more facilitative approach. As the students continue to assume an active role, the fourth and final stage, the *perform* stage—the synergistic classroom—is achieved, in which the consistency between the students' and instructor's respective new roles and ways of learning lead to enhanced teaching-learning performance.

Though this diagram illustrates a linear progression from a traditional classroom to a synergistic classroom, the actual movement from one stage to another is not so simple. In fact, faculty can expect a more nonlinear progression, characterized by fits and stops along the way.

Recognizing the Synergistic Classroom

Transforming a classroom from a traditional orientation to one that is consistent with the goals and opportunities associated with academic service learning is not easy. It takes an intentional campaign on the part of the instructor and lots of patience, because change will be far from immediate. If, however, the challenge is accepted and a commitment to experiment is made, how will one know when one has arrived at the synergistic stage?

For the most part, arrival will be self-evident to the faculty member. As Garry Hesser has written, "Every time faculty read students' papers, journals, exams, or *listen to the quality of discussion* [emphasis added] in a seminar, they are responsible for discerning whether learning is taking place" (1995, p. 35). Faculty will know. The most obvious dynamic to change will be the role of the students. An observer in a synergistic classroom will note that the students are actively engaged in discussion, among themselves or with the instructor. Discussion comfortably embraces both the content of academic readings and observations and experiences from the students' community placements. The instructor may be difficult to identify, though she or he might be seen facilitating the conversation to maximize the students' efforts to integrate the community-based and academic learning, contributing her or his own knowledge and relevant experiences to the discussion, or managing the discussion so that there is equal attention paid to the objective and subjective ways that students come to know. We might even see that if the instructor left the room, the level of learning would not be diminished.

In this classroom, discussion about theory and discussion about experiences is embraced by all, and efforts to integrate the two are made by all parties. The lines of distinction between the student role and the instructor role become blurred, so that students are teachers and learners, and instructors are learners as well as teachers. The traditional classroom's orientation toward individual student learning is replaced by a commitment to the learning of the collectivity. Questions and answers are perceived as equally important to the learning process, and ignorance, rather than to be avoided at all costs, is valued as a resource.

Once the synergistic classroom is achieved or at least approached, the new orientation to classroom teaching and learning can fan out to other components of the course. Faculty and students who have achieved the synergistic classroom will find that group academic projects, students reading each other's term papers, and final exams that call for bridging academic and community learning are consistent with the classroom transformation.

The Cost of the Synergistic Classroom: Time Away from Task?

Inevitably, the question arises: Does this effort to transform the classroom take time away from academic tasks? After all, time is expended in moving through stages 2 and 3 of the model, and, as acknowledged above, time on community learning necessarily takes time away from attention to theoretical learning. How does an instructor committed to student learning about an academic body of knowledge reconcile this dilemma?

The issue at hand has to do with the answer to the question: What is the task at hand in an academic course? If it is to impart as much information as possible, then the information-dissemination model unequivocally receives top honors. But if the task, in addition to learning content, is to excite and motivate students to learn during the course and after, to learn new ways of learning, and to develop a set of overall values in the field of study, then we know that the information-dissemination model is woefully lacking.

For example, one study found that while teachers are lecturing, students are not attending to what is being said 40 percent of the time (Pollio, 1984). Another study found that in the first ten minutes of lecture, students retain 70 percent of the information, but only 20 percent in the last ten minutes (McKeachie, 1986). Still another study found that four months after taking an introductory psychology course, students knew only 8 percent more than a control group who had never taken the course (Rickard, Rogers, Ellis, and Beidelman, 1988).

In contrast, we continually read faculty testimonials about the difference academic service learning has made in students' drive to learn (Bringle and Hatcher, 1996; Hammond, 1994; Hesser, 1995; Hudson, 1996; Kendrick, 1996; Yelsma, 1994). In a study conducted at the University of Michigan, students in sections of a political science class who were involved in community service as part of the course received better grades and reported more enhanced learning than their counterparts who were involved in library research (Markus, Howard, and King, 1993). In addition, they reported a statistically significant difference relative to their library research counterparts when asked about "performing up to my potential in this course," "developing a set of overall values in this field," and "learning to apply principles from this course to new situations."

A Formidable Challenge

As a relatively new and dilemma-filled pedagogy, academic service learning is not for the meek. Reformatting classroom norms, roles, and outcomes so that both academic and experiential learning can be joined requires a very deliberate effort around a rather formidable challenge. As a counternormative pedagogy, instructors who accept this challenge can expect initial resistance from students, periodic self-doubt about their own teaching accomplishments, and colleagues' looking askance upon this methodology. But the dividends—renewed motivation for learning by students, enhanced academic learning for students, renewed excitement for teaching by instructors, and better preparation of students for their roles as lifelong citizens and learners—will more than compensate for the effort.

References

Bringle, R. G., and Hatcher, J. A. "Implementing Service Learning in Higher Education." *Journal of Higher Education*, 1996, 67 (2), 221–239.

Chesler, M. A. "Community Service Learning as Innovation in the University." In J. Howard (ed.), *Praxis I: A Faculty Casebook on Community Service Learning*. Ann Arbor, Mich.: OCSL Press, 1993.

Freire, P. *Pedagogy of the Oppressed* (M. B. Ramos, trans.). New York: Continuum, 1970.

Hammond, C. "Integrating Service and Academic Study: Faculty Motivation and Satisfaction in Michigan Higher Education." *Michigan Journal of Community Service Learning,* 1994, *1*, 21–28.

Hesser, G. "An Assessment of Student Learning: Outcomes Attributed to Service-Learning and Evidence of Changes in Faculty Attitudes About Experiential Education." *Michigan Journal of Community Service Learning,* 1995, *2*, 33–42.

Honnet, E. P., and Poulsen, S. J. *Principles of Good Practice in Combining Service and Learning.* Wingspread Special Report. Racine, Wis.: The Johnson Foundation, 1989.

Howard, J. "Community Service Learning in the Curriculum." In J. Howard (ed.), *Praxis I: A Faculty Casebook on Community Service Learning.* Ann Arbor, Mich.: OCSL Press, 1993.

Hudson, W. E. "Combining Community Service and the Study of American Public Policy." *Michigan Journal of Community Service Learning,* 1996, *3*, 82–91.

Kendrick, J. R., Jr. "Outcomes of Service-Learning in an Introduction to Sociology Course." *Michigan Journal of Community Service Learning,* 1996, *3*, 72–81

Liu, G. "Knowledge, Foundations, and Discourse: Philosophical Support for Service-Learning." *Michigan Journal of Community Service Learning,* 1995, *2*, 5–18.

Markus, G., Howard, J. P. F., and King, D. C. "Integrating Community Service and Classroom Instruction Enhances Learning: Results from an Experiment." *Educational Evaluation and Policy Analysis,* 1993, *15* (4), 410–419.

McKeachie, W. *Teaching Tips: A Guidebook for the Beginning College Teacher.* (8th ed.) Lexington, Mass.: Heath, 1986.

Palmer, P. "Community, Conflict, and Ways of Knowing." In J. Kendall and Associates, *Combining Service and Learning: A Resource Book for Community and Public Service.* Vol. 1. Raleigh, N.C.: National Society for Internships and Experiential Education, 1990.

Pollio, H. *What Students Think About and Do in College Lecture Classes.* Teaching-Learning Issues no. 53. Knoxville: Learning Research Center, University of Tennessee, 1984.

Rickard, H., Rogers, R., Ellis, N., and Beidelman, W. "Some Retention, But Not Enough." *Teaching of Psychology,* 1988, *15*, 151–152.

Yelsma, P. "Combining Small Group Problem Solving with Service-Learning." *Michigan Journal of Community Service Learning,* 1994, *1*, 62–69.

JEFFREY P. F. HOWARD is assistant director for academic service learning at the Center for Learning through Community Service, University of Michigan. He is founder and editor of the Michigan Journal of Community Service Learning.

As a pedagogy for citizenship, service learning offers students the opportunity to experience and reflect on how citizens organize to bring their communities and their country closer to democracy.

A Pedagogy for Citizenship: Service Learning and Democratic Education

Meta Mendel-Reyes

Maria clutches the papers tightly. After over two hours of waiting through reports, announcements, awards, and other agenda items that seemed much less urgent than hers, the chance to speak has nearly arrived. She looks at the determined face of the African American woman seated beside her, one of several residents living across the street from a trash incinerator that has brought pollution, disease, noise, and rats to their quiet neighborhood. At last, they would have the opportunity to tell their story to elected officials who could do something about it. Maria glances down at the statistics that took her hours to research, hard data that would convince the county board of supervisors to act at last. As the chairman finally utters the words, "Time for public comment," she rises to her feet. Before she can open her mouth, the chairman slams down the gavel: "Meeting adjourned." As the supervisors file quickly out of the room, Maria stares in disbelief, her papers slipping from her hands to the floor. "We didn't even have our say!" she sputters. "How could they get away with it? Isn't this supposed to be a democracy?"

The scene of the county supervisors' meeting dissolves into the classroom at Swarthmore College, where the student and other members of her team have just finished reenacting this critical incident from their service learning experience in Political Science 19: "Democratic Theory and Practice." They point out that what happened at the meeting resembles a situation in one of the assigned readings, Gaventa's (1980) classic, *Power and Powerlessness: Quiescence and*

The writing of this chapter was supported by the National Academy of Education as part of a Spencer Postdoctoral Fellowship, 1996–1997.

Rebellion in an Appalachian Valley. Like the poor residents encountered by Maria, the miners in the book tried to raise their issue at a public hearing, only to be silenced. As a reading assignment, the power of a large corporation to control the political process seemed abstract, and perhaps even exaggerated, but as a lived experience, the threat to democracy could not be ignored.

After the class analyzes these two examples of power and powerlessness, the team tells them what the embattled residents did next. To ensure that their voices were heard, they marched, with the participation of the students, from the county building to their neighborhood. Local media covered the march extensively, helping to create a groundswell of support that ultimately convinced the city council to pass an historic resolution prohibiting any new waste disposal facilities that would increase pollution. The student team concludes that the residents had figured out how to make democracy work—by acting democratically.

The Democracy Project

The preceding scene occurred during my first year of teaching "Democratic Theory and Practice," one of three core courses in the Democracy Project at Swarthmore College. The Democracy Project is designed to deepen students' understanding and commitment to democratic citizenship in a multicultural society. "Citizenship" in this context refers to the rights and responsibilities that we share as members of a community, not to the privileged status of natives versus immigrants. Clearly, in an era of global xenophobia and ethnic cleansing, a new, less exclusionary definition of "citizenship" is needed.

The three core courses, "Democratic Theory and Practice," "Multicultural Politics," and "Community Politics: The Internship Seminar," all involve what we call community-based learning (service learning that emphasizes the mutual partnership between college and community). In the seminar, students engage in semester-long internships; the other two courses include a class community service day and further service learning options. Instead of being marginalized in the way that service learning often is, these courses are eligible for the college honors program and are taught by a tenure-track professor in the Department of Political Science (Mendel-Reyes, 1997).

Ironically, at the historic moment when formerly communist countries and dictatorships all over the world have embraced the example of American democracy, Americans themselves are turning their backs on civic life in increasing numbers. The challenge of democratic education in the United States at the end of the twentieth century is to teach young people not merely the skills of citizenship but also its value. The oldest and newest democracies share a goal: to encourage greater participation in the political process. From South Africa to the United States, service learning promises to revitalize citizenship education and citizenship itself by offering students the opportunity to learn and to practice the "what, how, and why" of democracy (Mendel-Reyes and Weinstein, 1996).

Democracy and Democratic Education

The word *democracy* joins the Greek words *demos*, "the people," and *kratia*, "rule," to form what seems to be a simple, straightforward concept: "the rule of the people." Yet since the dawn of political philosophy in classical Greece, theorists have argued over the meaning, the feasibility, and even the desirability of self-government. Plato ([ca 377 B.C.] 1941), arguably the first professor of citizenship, rejected the form of government under which his beloved teacher Socrates had been condemned to death. In Plato's eyes, the "people" were no more than an ignorant mob to be governed by "philosopher kings." Plato's best student, Aristotle ([ca 335–323 B.C.] 1971), disagreed, however, describing "man" as "a political animal," entitled and able to rule himself. Although the two sides have adopted various labels, their debate has continued to the present day. From the perspective of citizenship, the main issue is "participatory" versus "representative" democracy.

The Rule of the People? In participatory democracy, also called *civic republican* or *direct*, the people rule themselves literally by making decisions concerning their collective lives. What most of us today associate with citizenship, voting for others to make decisions for us, is less meaningful than making them to the extent possible ourselves. Because this model requires the full, active participation of all citizens in politics, it gives high priority to citizenship education. Democratic theorists from Tocqueville (1945) to Barber (1992) have argued that the health of democracy depends upon educating citizens in "schools of democracy," such as voluntary associations.

In representative democracy, sometimes referred to as *liberal* or *indirect*, the people select those who rule over them. Because this model envisions a passive role for most citizens, their education is less important than the training of an "elite" pool of potential representatives. Although some form of representation seems inevitable in today's large nations, most theorists of representative democracy neglect the critical question of how uneducated citizens can be expected to elect their leaders wisely and hold them accountable.

American political history can be viewed as a struggle between these two models of democracy and the corresponding approaches to citizenship and to citizen education. The Constitution, written by men who were deeply suspicious of the common people, signified the ascendence of the representative vision. The new form of government, with a complex system of checks and balances and separation of powers, was designed to prevent concerted action by a "tyrannical" majority (Madison, Hamilton, and Jay, 1961). The ideal and occasionally the reality of participatory citizenship remained alive throughout American history, however, surfacing most prominently during the great democratic movements of the late nineteenth and twentieth centuries, including the civil rights movement and the New Left during the 1960s (Mendel-Reyes, 1995). Today, near the end of the twentieth century, the conjunction of economic distress, social fragmentation, and political apathy has brought renewed attention to "our impoverished vision of citizenship" (Sandel, 1996, p. 57).

Meaningful participation often seems limited to that of distant bureaucracies and multinational corporations, who remain impervious to the actions of most national governments, let alone individual citizens. The power of the people has been further eroded by conflicts between natives and immigrants, whites and people of color, rich and poor.

Undemocratic Education. These antidemocratic trends in politics reflect and inform similar developments in education. Colleges and universities continue to give lip service to the ideal of knowledge for its own sake and the common good while struggling to cope with the reality that the academy has become increasingly exclusive, specialized, and corporate. Secondary and elementary schools are even more strapped for money and vision; finding enough chairs for students to sit upon inevitably becomes a higher priority than training them to be citizens.

In practice, if not in theory, there are two tracks of citizenship education in the United States. Schools separate the future citizenry into elite and mass, and the latter into skilled, unskilled, and unemployed workers (Rhoads and Valadez, 1996). For the masses, citizenship education is boring; dry textbooks, with endless charts of the three branches of government and "how a bill becomes a law," and rote assignments to memorize the Constitution and the Amendments are effective lessons in passivity. Despite the occasional mobility of individuals, active citizenship and economic security have become the privileges of a few rather than the rights of all.

A Pedagogy for Citizenship

The challenge of democratic education today is to teach students how to participate in a democracy that does not yet exist, and more, how to help to bring about that democracy. Like the pedagogy of popular education developed by the Brazilian educator Paulo Freire (1972), service learning connects personal and political transformation. Students transform themselves into citizens and their society into one that welcomes and promotes active citizenship.

Education for Democracy. In terms of the working definition of service learning developed for this book, "a pedagogical model that intentionally integrates academic learning and relevant community service," service learning as a pedagogy for citizenship integrates the academic study of democracy and the experience of democratic community service. The guiding principle behind the Democracy Project is that "the only truly effective education system for democracy is democracy—democratic action itself" (Lummis, 1996, p. 37). Through reflection upon the experience of democratic action, students are encouraged to expand the meaning of citizenship to include acting in a way that recognizes and promotes the citizenship of everyone.

It is important to recognize, however, that there is more than one legitimate approach to citizenship education, and that approaches need not be limited to programs that explicitly address citizenship. In fact, almost every service learning model that fits the working definition offers at least a minimal education in citizenship by exposing students to community life and to one facet of the citizen's role, service to the less fortunate. Moreover, it would be undemocratic to insist on a single definition of citizenship; if people are entitled to rule themselves, they are also entitled to decide how they wish to exercise their rule. It may well be that some will decide not to be politically active; the point is that it should be their choice. As citizens in a democracy, each of us should have the opportunity to participate in community decision making, and no one should have to depend indefinitely upon the service of others.

The "What and Why" of Democracy. The courses "Democratic Theory and Practice" and "Multicultural Politics" focus on the "what and why" of citizenship, whereas "Community Politics: The Internship Seminar" emphasizes the "how."

"Democratic Theory and Practice" explores the relationship between theories of democracy and the ways in which it is practiced in the United States, alternating between case studies, such as Gaventa's (1980), and theoretical works. The course includes two service learning assignments. Early in the semester, the class works together on a community service project, usually spending a Saturday morning helping a local group rehabilitate low-income housing. Each student also writes and presents a "theory in practice" report to the rest of the class, analyzing an individual experience of service during the semester.

"Multicultural Politics" investigates how racial, ethnic, and cultural diversity has shaped the American past and present, including the contested notion of democratic citizenship. Is the United States a melting pot, a mosaic, or a battleground of racial, ethnic, and cultural differences? The assigned texts include fiction and memoirs in voices that have often been ignored or silenced, along with history, social science, and journalism from a variety of perspectives. Students also draw on their own family histories and participate in a class community service project.

In both courses, service learning shows students the human face of controversial issues such as immigration, poverty, and environmental racism. Unlike many approaches to teaching social science, the Democracy Project does not reduce the recipients of service to the status of passive "problems" or helpless "victims." Instead, service learning offers students the opportunity to experience the ways in which people are organizing to improve their lives and to reclaim their rights as citizens. The key to this pedagogy for citizenship is reflection upon experience, upon what service learning teaches us about democracy, about difference, and about acting democratically in a multicultural society.

The "How" of Democracy. The heart of the Democracy Project is "Community Politics: The Internship Seminar," which explores democratic theory and multicultural politics at the community level through semester-long service internships. This course emphasizes the "how" of democracy: How do disempowered communities empower themselves? How can individual activists, from inside and outside the community, help to achieve democratic and multicultural political change? Students explore these questions by reflecting upon their internships in light of the readings and the dialogues with community activists, individually through their journals and other writing assignments, and as a class through discussion, small group work, and experiential exercises.

The students choose their internship from a list of potential placements with local service and advocacy organizations, preferably composed of and led by members of the community. These groups include the Chester Community Improvement Project, which rehabilitates abandoned houses and sells them to first-time buyers; Asian Americans United, which runs a youth leadership program for the diverse and growing Asian community of Philadelphia; and Chester Residents Concerned for Quality Living (CRCQL), the group of neighbors who have banded together to fight the trash incinerator.

At the beginning of each internship, the student, the supervisor from the host organization, and the instructor sign off on a "Community Involvement Agreement," which spells out expectations and responsibilities, including the intern's commitment to volunteer a minimum of five hours per week (sixty hours per semester). Signing this agreement also helps to set the tone of reciprocity—that the student does work needed by the community and the community provides knowledge and experience to the student in return (Kendall, 1990).

The seminar meets three hours each week and includes a meal, which we take turns in preparing. While eating, students go around the table sharing highlights from their internships; this is also the time to ask for help. Next is usually a dialogue with a community activist, followed by a more detailed presentation from one or two students each week about their internship experience. Students are encouraged to approach this assignment as a "teachable moment," an opportunity to convey something they have learned, or to probe more deeply into an aspect of community politics illuminated by their internships. In the last part of the seminar, we discuss issues raised by the readings, often in relation to themes that come up during the community or internship presentations.

For example, during a session with the president of CRCQL, a student expressed her reluctance to disagree with the people she encountered during her internship, since she was only an "outsider" in their community. The president responded, "Bring your brains!" because the community wants and needs the very best that volunteers have to offer. The ensuing discussion, which also brought in Martin Luther King's "Letter from a Birmingham Jail" (1964), deepened our reflections upon the challenge of serving in communities different from our own. As in this example, the plan for each seminar meeting is flexible and responsive to the students' concerns, another way in which the subject matter of democracy is woven into the design of the course.

Citizenship Skills. Building on "Democratic Theory and Practice" and "Multicultural Politics," the Internship Seminar integrates citizenship education as content with citizenship education as pedagogy. Students learn the skills of democracy—critical thinking, public deliberation, community-building, and collective action—by practicing them.

As a pedagogy for critical thinking, service learning provides opportunities for problem-posing; gathering evidence and analyzing it; and formulating, carrying out, and evaluating plans of action. In order to become critical thinkers, students must learn how to "question the answers!" (Vella, 1994, p. 28). Perhaps even more difficult, they must accept the fact that in this postmodern age there are few definitive answers to many of the most pressing questions facing communities (Rhoads, 1997).

For this reason, a pedagogy for critical thinking must also be a pedagogy for public deliberation. In the absence of certainty, political decisions are justified in large part by the quality of the process through which they were made. Through service learning, students improve their abilities to participate in democratic deliberation. The goal is more than simply learning how to express themselves verbally and in writing. Students are challenged to listen to a range of voices, to empathize with people different from themselves, and to compromise with others in the name of a common good that is often contested and tentative.

Community building, which service learning also teaches, strengthens the relationships that enable a member of a community to accept the results of public deliberation while retaining the capacity for critical thought. The Internship Seminar is designed to build community within the classroom as a way of studying community building outside of it. The shared meal, for example, helps to create an atmosphere that is less competitive than the typical classroom; it also demonstrates subtly that community does not just happen but must be built through ritual and effort. Our meals are often tasty lessons in multicultural politics because students enjoy preparing traditional meals from their own cultures.

To take collective action, the members of a community need to figure out ways to work together while acknowledging their differences, one of the most difficult lessons to learn in the classroom as well as in politics. Although they share a commitment to service, the twelve students enrolled in the Internship Seminar come from a range of racial, ethnic, and class backgrounds. Like many of their elders, they tend to equate "community" with harmony and resist the idea that democratic deliberation does not prevent or eliminate conflict. King's (1964) discussion of "creative tension" helps students to understand the positive uses of conflict as a catalyst for personal growth and the improvement of society. The instructor also encourages them to reflect upon how the members of their host organization resolve disputes among themselves.

Because not every "tension" is "creative," our deliberation within the classroom is structured to promote respect as well as the open expression of ideas and disagreements. For example, we take turns serving as the "vibes watcher"—the person who keeps an eye on the "vibes" of the group. The vibes watcher has the authority to jump in and call the group's attention to a range of feelings or behaviors that seem to interfere with learning, such as personal attacks, going off on a tangent, or even simple boredom.

Finally, service learning as a pedagogy for citizenship shows students that each of them can make a difference. Service learning increases their confidence as citizens, but not because their every experience of collective action is successful. Practicing democracy in the community, in a community organization, and in a classroom "community" is hard work and sometimes frustrating. However, service learning teaches students and their teachers how to learn from mistakes by engaging in a continuous sequence of action and reflection. Ultimately, the success of the Democracy Project will be measured by the extent to which its graduates continue to learn through service as they practice citizenship throughout the rest of their lives.

References

Aristotle. *The Politics of Aristotle* (E. Barker, ed. and trans.). London: Oxford University Press, 1971. (Originally published ca 335–323 B.C.)

Barber, B. R. *An Aristocracy of Everyone: The Politics of Education and the Future of America*. New York: Oxford University Press, 1992.

Freire, P. *Pedagogy of the Oppressed*. New York: Herder and Herder, 1972.

Gaventa, J. *Power and Powerlessness: Quiescence and Rebellion in an Appalachian Valley*. Urbana: University of Illinois Press, 1980.

Kendall, J. C. *Combining Service and Learning: A Resource Book for Community and Public Service*. Raleigh, N.C.: National Society for Internships and Experiential Education, 1990.

King, M. L., Jr. "Letter from a Birmingham Jail." In *Why We Can't Wait*. New York: New American Library, 1964.

Lummis, C. D. *Radical Democracy*. Ithaca, N.Y.: Cornell University Press, 1996.

Madison, J., Hamilton, A., and Jay, J. *The Federalist Papers* (C. Rossiter, ed.). New York: New American Library, 1961.

Mendel-Reyes, M. *Reclaiming Democracy: The Sixties in Politics and Memory*. New York: Routledge, 1995.

Mendel-Reyes, M. "Teaching/Theorizing/Practicing Democracy." In R. Battistoni and W. Hudson (eds.), *Service Learning in Political Science*. Washington, D.C.: American Association for Higher Education, 1997.

Mendel-Reyes, M., and Weinstein, J. "Community Service Learning as Democratic Education in South Africa and the United States." *Michigan Journal of Community Service Learning*, 1996, 3, 103–112.

Plato. *The Republic of Plato* (F. Cornford, trans.). London: Oxford University Press, 1941. (Originally published ca 377 B.C.)

Rhoads, R. *Community Service and Higher Learning: Explorations of the Caring Self*. Albany: State University of New York Press, 1997.

Rhoads, R. A., and Valadez, J. R. *Democracy, Multiculturalism, and the Community College: A Critical Perspective*. New York: Garland, 1996.

Sandel, M. J. "America's Search for a New Public Philosophy." *Atlantic Monthly*, 1996, 227 (3), 57–74.

Tocqueville, A. de. *Democracy in America*. New York: Knopf, 1945.·

Vella, J. *Learning to Listen, Learning to Teach: The Power of Dialogue in Educating Adults*. San Francisco: Jossey-Bass, 1994.

META MENDEL-REYES, a former labor and community organizer, teaches political science and directs the Democracy Project at Swarthmore College. She is author of Reclaiming Democracy: The Sixties in Politics and Memory.

The author discusses how critical multiculturalism informs service learning, providing a case study example of a student service project designed to work with homeless citizens.

Critical Multiculturalism and Service Learning

Robert A. Rhoads

"I learned that all people are innately afraid and that no one deserves to be without a voice and a safe place," explained Peter Johnson (a pseudonym) as he reflected on his experiences working with homeless citizens. He went on to add, "Stereotypes can be more damaging than can be fathomed." For Peter, his work in a soup kitchen in the nation's capital helped him to understand the strains of daily life faced by the homeless. The assumptions he once held about their lives were challenged by the conversations he had with homeless men and women. The "other" was not so distant, and people he once saw as strangers came to mean a little bit more in his own life. Peter's experiences also challenged how he thought about his major and what he could ultimately do with a degree in psychology. He openly wondered how he might be able to apply his learning to improve the lives of others. "I'm trying to figure out how these kinds of experiences fit into the rest of my life. I know that I can't see myself in a career where I'm not helping people in some way."

Peter highlights the kind of experiences students often have when professors put in the extra effort to help students connect their studies to community work. As many of the chapters in this volume demonstrate, service learning can have a powerful impact on students' lives as well as the lives of those they serve. For the students who participated in the Washington, D.C., project, few will ever forget the thrill of a homeless man who had his portrait sketched by an art student participating in the project. When she pulled the page from her tablet and handed it to him, his smile erased much of the social distance that economic circumstance had placed between them.

Although most service learning writers focus on how community service integrated with course work might help students to master academic material, some see another equally important goal of service learning: the role that students can play as change agents. This is poignantly captured in Chapter Four by Meta Mendel-Reyes. For students to see themselves as agents of social change, often it is necessary to have contact with diverse individuals and groups whose struggles might in some way connect to the lives of the students (Coles, 1993; Radest, 1993; Wuthnow, 1995). This was evident in Peter's case. Capturing the qualities of service learning that help to foster intimate connections with diverse others is the central concern of this chapter. To accomplish this goal, I call upon theories of multiculturalism.

Three Visions of Multiculturalism

In addressing the role that multiculturalism might play in shaping service learning, it is first necessary to clarify the meaning of the term itself. In general, three divergent philosophical positions of multiculturalism have shaped thinking about higher learning: conservative multiculturalism, mainstream multiculturalism, and critical multiculturalism (Bensimon, 1994; McLaren, 1995; Rhoads, 1995).

For some, the concept of multiculturalism calls attention to the pluralistic nature of U.S. society and raises questions about what courses and subjects might be added to the curricular offerings of colleges and universities. A conservative interpretation of multiculturalism tends to stress courses on diverse cultures as support offerings to be added to an already established canon. The traditional canon, which for the most part continues to represent the best of what Western civilization has produced, must not be replaced by faddish cultural perspectives. Instead, the canon simply needs a little spice to liven it up, and courses on diversity serve this purpose.

A second vision of multiculturalism may be described as "mainstream multiculturalism," for of the three visions, it has gained the strongest hold on the academy. From this perspective, multiculturalism is a means to achieve greater tolerance for diverse peoples. "By offering courses and educational experiences that expose students to a wide range of cultures and world views, both the majority and the minority will gain from increased understanding of the other" (Rhoads and Valadez, 1996, p. 8). Whereas conservative multiculturalism seeks to preserve the Western canon and simply include multiculturalism as an add-on to the primary curriculum, mainstream multiculturalism suggests that other worldviews are just as relevant as Western perspectives and that college students ought to become more familiar with and accepting of diverse cultures. In this manner, mainstream multiculturalism may be seen as part of the "human relations" project to create a more tolerant social environment.

Bensimon (1994) criticized the human relations view of multiculturalism because it downplays cultural differences: "It is primarily concerned with the reduction of tension and conflict among different groups. Accordingly, curricular change that is framed in human relations terms will focus on the development of more accepting attitudes" (p. 13). For Bensimon, merely "tolerating" diversity is problematic in that tolerance does not foster the kind of social transformation that enables diverse cultures intentionally to influence the academy as well as the larger society.

Conservative and mainstream multiculturalism fail to transform monocultural institutions into multicultural, democratic communities because they situate cultural diversity as subject matter to be learned or as diverse identities to be tolerated. Such views of multiculturalism are more accommodating than transformative. As McLaren (1995) wrote, "Multiculturalism without a transformative political agenda can just be another form of accommodation to the larger social order" (p. 126).

Bensimon (1994) favors a third vision that seeks social transformation based on diverse cultures and identities. A transformative version of multiculturalism has been described as critical multiculturalism because it combines the conditions of cultural diversity with the emancipatory vision of critical educational practice borrowing from postmodernism, critical theory, and feminism. This form of multiculturalism seeks to transform the academy from monolithic centers of power to democratic constellations in which organizational structures reflect a multiplicity of perspectives (Rhoads and Solorzano, 1995). Such a vision is compatible with liberatory forms of pedagogy in which a goal of education is to challenge students to become knowledgeable of the social, political, and economic forces that have shaped their lives and the lives of others (Freire, 1970; Giroux, 1992; hooks, 1994).

Instead of a college or university simply modifying its curriculum to include African American voices in a few of its courses or encouraging its majority students to be more tolerant of Chicana and Chicano students, the institution would go a step further and seek to reframe the organizational structure and culture by including diverse worldviews. Members of a university committed to critical multiculturalism might ask themselves: How can we rethink our admissions practices to reflect a commitment to diversity? How can faculty hiring processes be reframed if cultural diversity is of primary concern? How can we reconsider pedagogy around a more culturally inclusive agenda? For the purposes of this chapter, we would add: How might we think about service learning if a commitment to cultural diversity is a central concern? To answer the latter question, I introduce a case study of an intensive service learning project conducted in Washington, D.C.

The D.C. Project

For three consecutive years I volunteered with three separate groups of about 30–35 students and staff from Pennsylvania State University to work with homeless citizens in Washington, D.C., over winter breaks. During the course of each of these week-long service projects, we worked in various soup kitchens within the city, including Zacchaeus's Kitchen, So Others Might Eat, Mariam's Kitchen, and the Church of the Brethren Soup Kitchen. From these projects, I collected qualitative data about students and their interactions with homeless citizens. From this data, I highlight issues related to critical multiculturalism and its role in shaping service learning.

Coming to terms with cultural diversity involves much more than simply recognizing differences based on race or ethnicity. Cultural differences also exist when one examines social groups defined by age, gender, sexual orientation, or socioeconomic status. For example, much evidence suggests that males and females tend to adopt different strategies in constructing knowledge of their social worlds (Belenky, Clinchy, Goldberger, and Tarule, 1986; Gilligan, 1982). Similarly, lesbian, gay, and bisexual students face different challenges in negotiating college than heterosexual students (Rhoads, 1994). Also, age and maturity level have a major impact on a variety of educational and social experiences (Cross, 1981; Erikson, 1968; Ryff, 1991). In the D.C. project, the central issue of cultural diversity is socioeconomic status (SES). A concern with SES involves an analysis of differences in the lived experiences of homeless citizens and middle-class college students.

From the perspective of critical multiculturalism, relevant learning from the D.C. project is linked to students' understanding of the identities of homeless people and the kinds of social experiences they have. Though we most often think of knowledge of homeless lives as helpful information for students studying in the social sciences or helping professions, the reality is that through creative planning there are few majors that cannot be connected in some way to homelessness in particular and urban poverty in general. For example, as part of Howard University's team design project in engineering, a group of students developed an inflatable sleeping bag to be used by homeless citizens of D.C. Because the bag was inflatable and lightweight, it could be transported with an individual's belongings. To develop their project, the students had to understand some of the difficulties that homeless people face, such as dealing with cold temperatures and the need to transport possessions easily. The students accomplished this by holding discussions with homeless citizens and learning about their problems. Architectural students at another urban institution spent considerable time interacting with homeless citizens and then drafted designs for more affordable housing. As part of an ethics module of a civil engineering course at the Massachusetts Institute of Technology, students became involved in an urban neighborhood to better assess the potential impact that the construction of a new highway might have for this section of the city.

Although engaging in interactions with diverse others is an important aspect of a critical multicultural vision of service learning, there is much more to be expected of students. Simply understanding someone else's life is not enough to achieve the transformative goals of liberatory pedagogies such as critical multiculturalism. Students must also learn about the many ways that they might alter the circumstances of homeless citizens beyond the obvious path of providing a hot meal or a warm place to sleep. To get to this point, however, students often must first pass through a "personalizing" phase in which a diverse social group that they have only read about in a text book actually becomes "real" for them.

The service learning project in D.C. enabled students to learn about the lives of homeless people and in this way helped students to see homeless citizens as real people with real problems and concerns. For example, a senior majoring in management and journalism commented on what he thought was most significant about his work: "I enjoyed talking with a homeless man who had served in the Navy. But since then he had suffered a stroke and had paralysis on his left side. When I asked if he was in contact with his family back in Ohio where he was born, he said he was 'too gay' for them. He couldn't even recall the last time he had spoken to them." A junior majoring in health education also discussed what she thought was important about her experience: "My most significant learning experiences came from talking with some homeless people and trying to learn about their struggles. It was a real awakening for me to hear about their lives in great detail."

Other students reported similar experiences. A senior majoring in nursing participated in the D.C. project because she wanted to be able to better relate to and understand the problems of homeless people. She admittedly lacked knowledge of many of the issues and believed that personal interactions helped to educate herself. "One-on-one discussions with different homeless people was the most significant aspect of the project," she commented. "I realized that in part what they need is to be heard—to be able to share their experiences and feelings." A sophomore in sociology described an unforgettable moment she experienced on one of the repeat service trips to D.C.: "What sticks in my mind was meeting and remembering someone whom I had met in a soup kitchen last year and talking to him on a very deep and personal level. I think he remembered me too."

In terms of their interactions with homeless citizens, students involved in the project made several points. Some discussed becoming more empathetic with the plight of homeless citizens. One student elaborated, "I learned that the homeless in general do not earn their predicament. Instead, their problems are brought on by a series of events that are largely beyond their control. Such events could make myself or anyone wind up homeless." A junior majoring in psychology talked about how people often distance themselves from homeless people by making reference to "those people" as if they are somehow better than the homeless. This student also commented on how the service project had left her with a different view of the issues: "I feel entirely different about homeless people than I did previously. I understand better some of the circumstances that contribute to people losing their jobs, or their homes. But I also understand that many of the people I've met through this work are not helpless victims. They are more than capable of working and maintaining a normal life if there were just more opportunities."

Links to Academic Service Learning

Although the project discussed in this chapter was not directly tied to the formal curriculum of Pennsylvania State University, there is much that is applicable to academic service learning. For example, it is quite conceivable that an intense experience such as described here could be linked to a variety of courses and be held over a weekend or even during spring break. Students could have an option to participate in such a project, and it could easily be integrated with a variety of assigned readings. Liebow's (1993) sociological account of the lives of homeless women comes to mind. Coles's (1993) book on service and idealism and Barber's work on citizenship education are two more examples of texts that could be used to guide teaching related to a service project.

Liebow (1993) and many of the students involved in the D.C. project highlight the idea that the sharing of lives, of stories about other lives, is one way to make visible the experiences of another. When we truly learn about the lives and the problems others face, they become more real to us. A connection forms between the self and the other as our interdependence is uncloaked. Radest (1993) maintained that this is especially true when cultural differences exist among individuals involved in community service: "Community service is also built on assumptions of relationship. So, we assume that it is both possible and appropriate for culturally diverse persons to move, although not without difficulty, into each others' worlds and to have a shared world as well" (p. 114).

Radest talked about how service is one way to help overcome the "lost connection"—the sense of community that seems to have eroded in today's technologically advanced, postmodern society. Radest did not suggest that building lost connections is about erasing cultural difference and returning to a mythical America of the past grounded in homogeneity and harmony. Instead, overcoming our sense of alienation involves recognizing real differences and at the same time understanding that we can build some common connections—that the stranger is not so different from myself and that we can engage together in a common struggle or cause. The life of the diverse "other" has much to offer to the "self."

Thus, from a critical multicultural perspective, cultural difference is not to be situated as an obstacle to building community (Tierney, 1993). Instead, through activities such as service learning, diversity becomes a vehicle through which we learn and share with one another and build connections in the process.

The kind of community building and social transformation stressed by theories such as critical multiculturalism demand an intentional pedagogical effort on the part of educators. For example, during each of the D.C. trips we stayed in the basement of a church on the corner of Fourth Street and Independence Avenue (in the southeast quadrant of D.C.), just a few blocks from the Capitol building. Students and staff worked in teams to prepare our own meals and carry out various cleaning chores around the church. A typical day involved getting up at 5 or 6 A.M., eating breakfast, and then taking public transportation or a university van to one of the many soup kitchens within the city. Most groups returned to the church by 5 P.M., at which time a team prepared and then served dinner. After dinner, there was a series of small-group activities, often involving extensive reflection and discussion of issues related to service and homelessness. Social service and volunteer workers from the D.C. area were invited to stop by and give perspective to some of the complex problems associated with urban poverty. One entire day was spent visiting legislators at the Capitol and meeting with activists involved in political, economic, and social issues connected with homelessness. The point I want to stress is that there was an intentional effort to link students' experiences to larger social issues and a hope that the project might inspire them to become agents of social change.

The importance of intentionality in planning the community service components of academic service learning cannot be stressed enough. To ignore the possible connections between course material and the service experience will result in two failures: A lack of intentionality will not help students to connect course work to community service, and it likely will not foster the kind of connection students need to make between theory and practice. As Freire (1970) argued, helping students to connect theory to action is a necessary component of liberatory forms of pedagogy.

Service learning grounded in critical multiculturalism must always ask the big questions: Why do we have significant economic gaps between different racial groups? Why do women continue to face economic and social inequities? Why does the richest country on earth have such a serious problem with homelessness? Indeed, critical multiculturalism as a guide to service learning offers a powerful educational option that college and university professors can bring to the teaching and learning enterprise.

References

Belenky, M. F., Clinchy, B. M., Goldberger, N. R., and Tarule, J. M. *Women's Ways of Knowing: The Development of Self, Voice, and Mind.* New York: Basic Books, 1986.

Bensimon, E. M. (ed.). *Multicultural Teaching and Learning.* University Park, Pa.: National Center on Postsecondary Teaching, Learning, and Assessment, 1994.

Coles, R. *The Call of Service: A Witness to Idealism.* Boston: Houghton Mifflin, 1993.

Cross, K. P. *Adults As Learners.* San Francisco: Jossey-Bass, 1981.

Erikson, E. H. *Identity: Youth and Crisis.* New York: Norton, 1968.

Freire, P. *Pedagogy of the Oppressed* (M. B. Ramos, trans.). New York: Continuum, 1970.

Gilligan, C. *In a Different Voice: Psychological Theory and Women's Development.* Cambridge, Mass.: Harvard University Press, 1982.

Giroux, H. A. *Border Crossings: Cultural Workers and the Politics of Education.* New York: Routledge, 1992.

hooks, b. *Teaching to Transgress: Education as the Practice of Freedom.* New York: Routledge, 1994.

Liebow, E. *Tell Them Who I Am: The Lives of Homeless Women.* New York: Penguin Books, 1993.

McLaren, P. *Critical Pedagogy and Predatory Culture.* New York: Routledge, 1995.

Radest, H. *Community Service: Encounter with Strangers.* New York: Praeger, 1993.

Rhoads, R. A. *Coming Out in College: The Struggle for a Queer Identity.* New York: Bergin & Garvey, 1994.

Rhoads, R. A. "Critical Multiculturalism, Border Knowledge, and the Canon: Implications for General Education and the Academy." *Journal of General Education,* 1995, *44* (4), 256–273.

Rhoads, R. A., and Solorzano, S. M. "Multiculturalism and the Community College: A Case Study of an Immigrant Education Program." *Community College Review*, 1995, 23 (2), 3–16.

Rhoads, R. A., and Valadez, J. R. *Democracy, Multiculturalism, and the Community College: A Critical Perspective*. New York: Garland, 1996.

Ryff, C. D. "Possible Selves in Adulthood and Old Age: A Tale of Shifting Horizons." *Psychology and Aging*, 1991, 6 (2), 286–295.

Tierney, W. G. *Building Communities of Difference: Higher Education in the Twenty-First Century*. New York: Bergin & Garvey, 1993.

Wuthnow, R. *Learning to Care: Elementary Kindness in an Age of Indifference*. New York: Oxford University Press, 1995.

ROBERT A. RHOADS is assistant professor in the Department of Educational Administration at Michigan State University. He is author of Community Service and Higher Learning: Explorations of the Caring Self *and* Freedom's Web: Student Activism in an Age of Cultural Diversity.

Through his service learning assignment, Rudy learns to pose new questions about his old habits of thought. He learns the important difference between an opinion passionately held and a problem that needs to be solved. He learns to think and reflect critically.

Reading, Writing, and Reflection

David D. Cooper

"What really irked me about Betty's decision," Rudy writes in his journal, "was that it should have been an editorial decision based on layout, design balance, etc. Instead, it was based on a phony rationale. The incident had an adverse effect on my outlook towards service at the Center." Rudy explains:

> When Betty and I discussed the final edits for the newsletter, she also explained to me that there was to be a change in the layout: [U.S.] Senator [Spencer] Abraham would not have his picture included in his story [about renaissance zones in Michigan]. Another individual, Flint Mayor Woodrow Stanley, had just sent a photo of himself to accompany his article. Mayor Stanley happens to be Black. Since Newt Gingrich's photo was already running with his story [on the Earning by Learning program Gingrich founded for inner-city youngsters], it would be "more balanced" if we ran a photo of the Black gentleman and withheld Abraham's, providing an element of diversity. . . . I am simply tired of hearing we should/should not do something based on the color of a person's skin. This type of action does nothing to advance the fight against discrimination. It is a way for those in charge to give the appearance of a diversified newsletter. . . . This one incident affected my outlook on the service I was doing.

As part of a required service learning component for his general education writing class, Rudy chose an assignment as newsletter assistant at his university's outreach office for economic development and urban affairs, where he works closely with Betty, editing articles that appear in the Center's monthly newsletter. The community placements chosen for students in Rudy's class were carefully selected as good sites for "real time" writing projects that address tangible and responsive audiences and link writing in a field of the student's choosing—in Rudy's case, public administration—with formal classroom-based writing activities and instruction. In addition to writing for an agency, students are required to keep a written journal record that functions both as further writing practice and, more important, as opportunities for students to reflect critically and systematically on their service experiences.

In his next journal entry, Rudy relates an incident that has no ostensible bearing on diversity policy. At the prompting of his teacher, Rudy chooses instead to write about Betty herself, seeking some insight into her personality and the character of her commitment.

> As we were leaving the Center last Tuesday so that Betty could give me a ride home, the family that lives next door to the Center arrived home. They were obviously an economically disadvantaged family, since they lived in a less affluent part of the city. As Betty was getting in the car, the little girl from next door called her name and came racing over. Immediately Betty gave the little girl a big hug, and asked about her day at school, etc. This scene may have had nothing to do with my work, and it may have been just a minor event in the grand scheme of things, but it touched me. Here was a woman that was so compassionate and caring, and here was a little girl who respected and appreciated this relationship so much. It really gave me a bit of insight into Betty's nature. It became clear why she was working at the Center. She was inherently a person with a great deal of love to give. That's simply a part of her make-up, and it was evidenced by this scene. One could tell that Betty truly believed that nothing, not even a poor economic situation, could hinder this young girl's future. And I think I felt the same.

Even though Rudy takes pains to point out that the scene in the driveway "may have had nothing to do with my [actual] work," it still has powerful resonance for his attitude toward service and the legitimacy of his service-learning assignment at the Center. Indirectly, even covertly, Rudy's discovery of the depth and authenticity of Betty's commitment to economic justice surely complicates, as his teacher may have hoped, that attitude of certainty he had earlier used to dismiss Betty's editorial decision as partisan and politically motivated.

Structuring Critical Reflection: The Critical Incident Journal

The journals that Rudy and his classmates kept are modeled on the critical incident journal format devised by Stanton (1995). The "critical incident" technique differs from more traditional journal narratives in several ways. Primarily, as Stanton explains to students, "Rather than [providing] a descriptive record of daily life, a critical incident journal includes detailed analysis of only those incidents which change you or your perspective on your service experience. . . . Rather than simply describing and interpreting an incident and the people involved," Stanton continues, "this reflective technique enables [you] to use the incident and its impact as a means for self-monitoring and personal exploration" (p. 59). In addition to identifying an event and describing its relevant details, the critical incident journal format requires students to pursue the three rhetorical steps of description, analysis, and reflection.

Step 1. Describe your role in the incident. What did you do? How did you react? How did others react?

Step 2. Analyze the incident. How well or how poorly did you understand the situation? Was your reaction—or the reaction of others—well informed or based on misinformation? How did you handle it? What would you do differently next time?

Step 3. What impact did the incident have on you? Why do you view it as "critical"? How has the incident influenced your feelings about working at your placement site? What have you learned? How has your perspective on yourself or others been changed and/or reinforced? Where do you go from here?

When responding to his first journal entry, Rudy's teacher notes that he describes the incident surrounding Betty's photo layout decision with precision and good detail, but his reaction to it, she suggests, may be more emotive ("What really irked me . . .") than critically reflective. She encourages him either to revisit the incident in another entry or select a new incident to write about with special attention to fleshing out Step 3. Rudy's teacher also wisely defers direct comment on Rudy's conclusion that the episode over the picture layout evidences a phony diversity policy. Nor does she broach the issue of Rudy's boilerplate conservatism, a political alignment he had proudly and skillfully underscored in earlier journal entries as though itching to provoke her own liberalism. Instead, she focuses on the way Rudy "bookends" his journal entry with references to unarticulated changes in attitude. She encourages Rudy to spell out the exact changes in his outlook toward service brought about by the incident. In an effort to redirect his antagonism, she also urges him to write about another incident at the Center that either confirms or perhaps confounds his strong belief that Betty's editorial decision grew out of a bogus rationale for racial diversity.

With the help of the critical incident format, Rudy's teacher provides new conditions and ramifications that seek to redirect Rudy's natural powers of curiosity into investigations that are more intellectually responsible and more critically engaged. In doing so, she seizes on the rival interpretations that open Rudy's first passage to critical scrutiny—what John Dewey (1933) called "the strife of alternative interpretations" (p. 121). It may not be enough, she suggests, to be "simply tired of hearing" about racial diversity. She persists in posing questions that push Rudy to think in new ways, to reflect critically, and to question his own perceptions of what he considers a critical incident at the Center. Why, for example, should one choose pictures for a newsletter based on typographic considerations alone? Do race-based editorial decisions over layout send important and defensible messages to readers in support of diversity? Which of these competing interpretations has the rightful claim? What implications, she hints, might that "rightful claim" have for Betty's integrity?

Transforming Values Through Reflection

The narrative development between Rudy's two journal entries—from static indignation to dynamic reaffirmation, from annoyance to rectitude—captures, in fact, what Dewey considered as the primary function of reflective thought: "to transform a situation in which there is experienced . . . conflict [or] disturbance of some sort, into a situation that is clear, coherent, settled, harmonious. . . . Genuine thinking winds up, in short, with an appreciation of new values" (1933, pp. 100–101).

It is important to point out that Rudy continues to write favorably about articles and opinions advancing the conservative agenda. "The key to turning around the urban disadvantaged," he later writes, "lies in programs that promote rugged individualism, rather than encouraging people to expect a handout." His curiosity and powers of inquiry shift, however, to the moral integrity of those who act on behalf of policy and away from the validity or political viability of the policies themselves. Rudy's political conservatism begins to expand and take on a communitarian ring—once again illustrating Dewey's belief that "all reflective thinking is a process of detecting relations" (1933, p. 77). For example, Rudy writes that "one can show their [sic] compassion by forming ideas . . . such as [about how] people help themselves," and that urban renewal policies must "provide a greater good: helping the community as a whole." His new interests in moral consensus and the common good, moreover, reveal the kinds of social attitudes that naturally grow out of reflective thought and, as Dewey further believed, are indispensable to the nurture of democracy and responsible citizenship.

"The clear consciousness of a communal life, in all its implications," according to Dewey, "constitutes the idea of democracy" (Robertson, 1992, p. 341). That clarifying consciousness can be seen in Rudy's willingness to reevaluate his beliefs in light of Betty's different attitude about photo layout and diversity, Rudy's reconsideration of public policy in terms of the community as a whole, and ultimately (what he may have been most "touched by" when the child raced over to embrace Betty) his realization that one's own good cannot be easily separated from the good of others.

In many respects, Rudy's experience at the Center encapsulates a tension among service learning educators and practitioners that is best resolved through the use of structured critical reflection exercises and techniques like the critical incident journal. Should Rudy's teacher, to put it bluntly, set out to redirect, indeed redress, his political and social conservatism? Or is Rudy's social consciousness incidental to the academic work going on at the intersection of his assignment at the Center and his enrollment in a writing class at his university? What is the proper character, in other words, of her intervention? Should the goal of a service-learning-infused curriculum be the preparation of students like Rudy for social action skills? Or should the goal be to develop intellectual competence and working knowledge in service of students' courses of academic study? To track Rudy's learning curve along separate social and cognitive spectra may beg, however, the wrong questions. Rudy's case may suggest that solving social problems vis-à-vis active community involvement and engaging intellectual processes may be more complementary than polarized. Rudy simultaneously learns to apply critical intelligence to his political beliefs while he engages in a practice of building democratic awareness and democratic community at the Center. He submits his political beliefs to the stimulus of critical reflection, not to a political litmus. He learns to formulate new questions about old habits of thought. He learns the important difference between an opinion passionately felt and powerfully held and a problem that needs to be solved and for which answers must be sought. He undergoes what Kolb (1984) describes as "learning [that] transforms . . . impulses, feelings, and desires . . . into higher-order purposeful action" (p. 22). If anything, ideology loses its exclusive and unchallenged grip on Rudy's political conservatism. His passion for rugged individualism now carries an ethical valence that transforms it into a more socially responsive conservatism: a conservatism, it could be said, with an articulate moral philosophy.

In the development of his narrative reflections, Rudy discovers that a valuation he previously held no longer works well for him. He could no longer satisfactorily dismiss Betty's editorial decision as politically motivated and, as such, rooted shallowly in ideological ground. He begins instead to experiment with alternative modes of valuation based on ethical and moral criteria and then to test those criteria experimentally to find out whether a life, as well as social policy, can be guided more satisfactorily according to them. Rudy is clearly more moved by the Betty who elicits the child's tender affections than he is by the Betty who makes an editorial decision based on racial balance. Given his teacher's encouragement to rethink his beliefs through the encounter with someone who believes differently, Rudy learns more about diversity—its complexity, its interpersonal ramifications, its socioethical consequences, its rootedness in the common good—than he could have in weeks of reading and classroom discussion alone.

Experiential Roots of Reflective Thinking

In a word, Rudy undergoes what several generations of modern educational theorists, beginning with Dewey and cresting in the more recent work of Kolb, refer to formally as an experiential learning cycle that is driven, in large part, by the adaptive learning modality of reflective observation. Arguing for the reflexive nature of learning processes, Kolb (1984) acknowledges the dynamic spiral character of knowledge formation and its anchorage in a student's concrete, lived experience. Rudy's service learning assignment at the Center provides a good case for what Dewey and Kolb view as the "situatedness of reflective thinking" (Dewey, 1933, p. 99) that is both the indispensable agent and the object of knowledge formation. Follow the thread of an idea or "the stuff of knowledge far enough," Dewey writes, "and you will find some situation that is directly experienced, something undergone, done, enjoyed, or suffered, and not just thought of. Reflection is occasioned by the character of this primary situation. It does not merely grow out of it" (1933, p. 99).

Reflective thinking is not only an organic component in the learning cycle, it is simultaneously the very ground from which knowledge and belief spring. Reflective thinking, in short, is both process and product. As such, reflective thinking has become a key subject in the massive literature of experiential learning theory and, more recently, the operational linchpin of contemporary service learning pedagogy (Boud, Keogh, and Walker, 1984; King and Kitchener, 1994; Silcox, 1993).

Theoretical Foundations of Reflective Thinking

Dewey (1933) presents one of the most durable cases, as Kolb (1984) acknowledges, for the critical primacy of structured reflective thinking in the educative process. Together with other significant works, Dewey (1916, 1938) left an intellectual legacy that best articulates that educative process through the guiding principles of experiential learning, including the cultivation and expression of a student's individuality, the transformation of the classroom into a venue for free and independent activity, inquiry, and thought, and the importance of learning through experience. Growing out of his abiding faith in the scientific method and experimentalism and his deep dedication to radical democracy as the model for progressive education, Dewey argues that reflective thinking is both the means and end that should be cultivated by education, properly considered.

Dewey defines reflective thinking succinctly as "active, persistent and careful consideration of any belief or supposed form of knowledge in the light of the grounds that support it and the further conclusions to which it tends" (1933, p. 9). Extending his definition into the sphere of pedagogical practice, Dewey argues that reflective thought results from "careful and extensive study, . . . purposeful widening of the area of observation [under study], . . .[and] reasoning out the conclusions of alternative conceptions to see what would follow in case one or the other were adopted for belief" (1933, p. 8). For Dewey, reflective thinking is essential to the pragmatic application of the scientific attitude and outlook to human life and education. It therefore encompasses *cognitive processes* such as the logical management of an orderly chain of ideas to a controlling purpose and end, *social or democratic functions* called upon when public conflicts demand resolution through common problem solving and effective public discourse, and the *ethical skills* that Dewey adopts as the ground of reflective thinking: open-mindedness, whole-heartedness, and intellectual responsibility.

Reflective thinking is always inaugurated by what Dewey calls a "forked-road" situation in which a student faces an ambiguous dilemma that confronts him or her with the reliability and the worth of a previously held belief. "Difficulty or obstruction," Dewey continues, "in the way of reaching a belief brings us . . . to a pause. In the suspense of uncertainty[,] . . . demand for the solution of a perplexity is the steadying and guiding factor in the entire process of reflection" (1933, p. 14). Kolb synthesizes Dewey's point into one of the central premises of current experiential learning theory. "The process of learning," Kolb (1984) states, "requires the resolution of conflicts between dialectically opposed modes of adaptation to the world" (p. 29). Kolb is quick to add that "reflective observation abilities" are indispensable agents in that experience of adaptation.

Dewey takes pains to break down that process of engaging a dilemma into multiple aspects or "terminals" of reflective activity that span three progressive stages: problematization, hypothesis formation, and testing of the hypothesis. "Reflective thinking," Dewey summarizes, "involves (1) a state of doubt, hesitation, perplexity, mental difficulty, in which thinking originates, and (2) an act of searching, hunting, inquiring, to find material that will resolve the doubt, settle and dispose of the perplexity" (1933, p. 12). The movement from doubt to the disposition of a perplexity is engendered, first and foremost, by what Dewey insists are the critical conditions under which students must work and learn: "the provision of a real situation that arouses inquiry, suggestion, reasoning, testing, etc." (p. 283). This emphasis on the situatedness of reflective observation and its centrality to the learning process leads to a statement of Kolb's that has become a widely quoted catch phrase of the contemporary experiential learning movement: "Learning is the process whereby knowledge is created through the transformation of experience" (1984, p. 38).

Practicing Critical Reflection

Among the many successful efforts to render Dewey and Kolb's theories of reflective thinking into practical classroom application (Silcox, 1993; Goldsmith, 1995), Eyler, Giles, and Schmiede's 1996 *A Practitioner's Guide to Reflection in Service-Learning* stands out as particularly illuminating and incisive. They succeed in putting theory into practice, but, more important, their guide to reflection activities and techniques grows out of hundreds of structured interviews with students across the country enrolled in service learning courses. "The experiences of the students we encountered through this study," the authors write, emphasize "that reflection is the glue that holds service and learning together to provide [optimal] educative experiences" (p. 16).

The authors' research indicates that there are four principal criteria for successful application of reflective thinking to students' service learning experiences. They compress these criteria into "the 4 C's of reflection." "Over the course of this study," they conclude, "certain themes have reappeared repeatedly as critical factors in effective reflective activity. The best reflection is *Continuous* in time frame, *Connected* to the 'big picture' information provided by academic pursuits, *Challenging* to assumptions and complacency, and *Contextualized* in terms of design and setting" (p. 21).

In using their interview data to structure reflection guidelines, Eyler, Giles, and Schmiede stress that reflection activities must flex according to various student learning styles. After all, students "learn to learn" in different ways. Therefore, faculty and coordinators involved with service learning should ideally offer a variety of reflection activities that accommodate differences across the range of student learning styles, which Eyler, Giles, and Schmiede identify as *activists, reflectors, theorists,* and *pragmatists.* In addition, the authors offer a "Reflection Activity Matrix" that reminds service-minded educators just how integral critical reflection is to other learning activities and modalities.

From Expectation to Experience

As service learning practitioners themselves, Eyler, Giles, and Schmiede realize that the most important element in effective reflection is also the most difficult and problematic for teachers to implement successfully: the challenge of pushing students to think critically and to engage issues in a more critically reflective way. Challenging reflection involves a hard balancing act. A teacher must be willing to intervene, pose tough questions, and propose often uncomfortable points of view for a student's consideration. A teacher must also be ready to back off and give support in order to nurture the independence and autonomy that are the lifeblood of experiential learning processes. Revisiting Rudy's service learning experience may suggest that achieving this balance is not strictly a matter of adopting frameworks and guidelines or following rules, but it is more a question of taking what service learning practitioners recognize as the path to critical learning: "Learning is best conceived as a process . . . grounded in experience, not in terms of outcomes," as Kolb puts it, and "a process . . . continuously modified by experience" (1984, pp. 26–27). In other words, a good teacher is prepared to set his or her students upon a journey to knowledge, and then be willing to go along for the ride.

Returning to Rudy's service learning assignment at the Center, much to his own credit he sets out to inquire into the meaning of what he learns and what difference it may have to his conservative beliefs. That search for meaning begins in Dewey's "forked-road" situation and it follows, as predicted by Kolb, a trajectory of transformation. On the one hand, Betty's editorial decision initially demonstrates to Rudy that diversity is only a matter of "appearances." Therefore, he is inclined to dismiss Betty's actions as arbitrary. But given the interpersonal realities Rudy faces in his actual working relationship at the Center (because his learning process is situated and grounded in lived experience), does it follow, as logically perhaps it must, that *Betty is an arbitrary person?* Should he not respect her?

Rudy's teacher occasions the ambiguity by inviting Rudy to probe into the implications that Betty's layout decision has for changes in his attitudes about working at the Center. He must squarely face the antagonism he writes about in his journal over this incident against the great enthusiasm he has when returning to work at the Center—for Rudy continues to speak about how "stimulating" his service has been and how he is "gaining a better understanding of the nuts and bolts of editing a newsletter . . . while also looking at

Michigan's distressed communities and ways to revitalize them." Rudy's teacher also positions Rudy in such a way that he has to confront and work through some unstated assumptions he might be making. Is Betty an enforcer of orthodoxy? And what about the Mayor of Flint? Were it not for the color of his skin, would he deserve his picture on the newsletter cover? Paraphrasing Dewey, Rudy's teacher seizes on the real possibilities the incident harbors for Rudy to examine his assumptions more carefully and extensively, to widen the area of his inquiry into a cherished belief, and to follow his reasoning all the way to conclusions and alternatives he had not before considered due to the narrow depth of field compassed by his initial dismissal of Betty's decision as biased and unfair. Rudy's teacher problematizes his strongly held belief that diversity is a matter of "appearances" alone and "does nothing to advance the fight against discrimination." She provides impetus to Rudy's formation of a hypothesis concerning whether Betty's diversity policy is only skin-deep. Rudy tests the hypothesis. He probes into the reliability of a belief that once seemed so indisputable and obvious, and he finds it wanting in light of his discovery of Betty's real passion for community.

Rudy's learning occurs right at the place Kolb (1984) describes as "the interplay between expectation and experience," an interplay mediated by reflective thinking. Dewey (1933) reminds us that, like Rudy, we all have the tendency to believe that which is in harmony with desire. We take that to be true which we should like to have so, and contrary ideas have difficulty gaining lodgment. We draw weak conclusions as we fail to examine and test our ideas because of personal attitudes. When we generalize, we tend to make sweeping assertions based on only a few cases. Observation also reveals the powerful force wielded by social influences that have actually nothing to do with the truth or falsity of what is asserted and denied. As such, Kolb wisely concludes, "If the education process begins by bringing out the learner's beliefs and theories, examining them and testing them, and then integrating the new, more refined ideas into the person's belief systems, the learning process," as in Rudy's case, "will be facilitated" (1984, p. 27).

References

Boud, D., Keogh, R., and Walker, D. (eds.). *Reflection: Turning Experience into Learning.* New York: Routledge, 1984.

Dewey, J. *Democracy and Education.* New York: Free Press, 1916.

Dewey, J. *How We Think.* New York: Heath, 1933.

Dewey, J. *Experience and Education.* New York: Collier, 1938.

Eyler, J., Giles, D. E., and Schmiede, A. *A Practitioner's Guide to Reflection in Service-Learning: Student Voices and Reflections.* Nashville, Tenn.: Vanderbilt University, 1996.

Goldsmith, S. *Journal Reflection: A Resource Guide for Community Service Leaders and Educators Engaged in Service Learning.* Washington, D.C.: The American Alliance for Rights and Responsibilities, 1995.

King, P. M., and Kitchener, K. S. *Developing Reflective Judgment: Understanding and Promoting Intellectual Growth and Critical Thinking in Adolescents and Adults.* San Francisco: Jossey-Bass, 1994.

Kolb, D. A. *Experiential Learning: Experience As the Source of Learning and Development.* Englewood Cliffs, N.J.: Prentice Hall, 1984.

Robertson, E. "Is Dewey's Educational Vision Still Viable?" *Review of Research in Education,* 1992, *18,* 335–381.

Silcox, H. C. *A How-to Guide to Reflection: Adding Cognitive Learning to Community Service Programs.* Philadelphia: Brighton Press, 1993.

Stanton, T. K. "Writing About Public Service: The Critical Incident Journal." In M. Ford and A. Watters (eds.), *Guide for Change: Resources for Implementing Community Service Writing.* New York: McGraw-Hill, 1995.

DAVID D. COOPER is associate professor of American thought and language in the American Studies Program at Michigan State University and founder of The Service-Learning Writing Project.

Participatory action research has emerged as a popular form of service learning in distressed urban and rural communities. The successful development of a community-owned farmers' market in East St. Louis, Illinois, illustrates the principles, methods, and challenges of this approach to social science and community action.

Participatory Action Research as Service Learning

Kenneth M. Reardon

Public and private colleges and universities have been subjected to a steady stream of criticism throughout the 1990s, both for a lack of research that addresses our major environmental, economic, and social problems and for a failure to prepare graduates fully to meet the challenges of socially responsible citizenship.

Increasing numbers of colleges and universities are responding by encouraging faculty to incorporate community service learning in their teaching and research. By doing so, students have the opportunity to acquire important new knowledge, skills, and civic competencies while providing services to distressed urban and rural communities. Several major universities, including Providence College, Portland State University, and Rutgers University, have gone so far as to make participation in service learning a requirement for baccalaureate graduation.

The establishment of ongoing university-community partnerships is one means through which educational institutions have attempted to enrich students' educational experiences and encourage faculty to conduct research relevant to the community. Although faculty, students, and administrators have a growing interest in partnerships with communities, community residents and leaders have not always shared this enthusiasm. Too many past projects with universities have generally provided more resources for the campus than the local community, a situation perceived as evidence of an unequal partnership. When university research into the causes of social problems does not also address potential solutions, it is viewed by the community as meeting campus research goals without responding to community needs. The *professional-expert* research model, which restricts community input, still dominates most campus-community partnerships. In addition, leaders in low-income communities are painfully aware of the role local colleges and universities often play in promoting uneven patterns of development through their policies regarding labor, investment, purchasing, property management, and land acquisition.

In seeking to overcome these obstacles to resident involvement in local service learning projects, university scholars are increasingly adopting participatory action research methods (Hall, 1993). This emerging research paradigm seeks to enhance the problem-solving capacities of community participants by actively involving residents, business leaders, and elected officials in every phase of the research along with the university-trained professionals (Whyte, 1991).

Historical Antecedents

Three distinctive bodies of work laid the foundation for the emergence of participatory action research as a major new social science paradigm and methodology for social change in the United States in the 1980s and 1990s (Whyte, Greenwood, and Lazes, 1991). The first was the development of mutual self-help networks among subsistence farmers in Tanzania and other developing countries in the mid–1970s as an alternative to the largely unsuccessful United Nations–funded "Green Revolution" that featured top-down agricultural technology transfer projects from the northern to the southern hemisphere. The second was the creation of a series of labor/management committees on industrial competitiveness and innovation initially organized by Einor Thursrud of the Norwegian Industrial Democracy Project and later by Eric Trist of the Tavistock Institute. The third was the proliferation in the United States of tactical research activities by direct action organizing projects representing low-income families inspired by the grassroots organizing and empowerment philosophy of the late Saul Alinsky (Boyte, Booth, and Max, 1986). These efforts led to the development of a highly participatory form of community research in the 1980s that integrated the "local" knowledge of those most affected by a social issue with the "expert" knowledge of university-trained professionals to create innovative solutions to society's most intractable social problems (Argyris, Putnam, and Smith, 1985).

One of the earliest examples of a successful university-based participatory action research project took place in the mid–1970s when Eric Trist from the University of Pennsylvania and William F. Whyte from Cornell University assisted local labor leaders, plant managers, and municipal officials of Jamestown, New York, in an effort to reverse the decline of their region's fine furniture industry (Meek, Nelson, and Whyte, 1983). Scholars were particularly interested in this highly collaborative community assistance effort in light of the perceived failure of the professional-expert model of urban research in which outside consultants, who often have little prior knowledge of the community being studied, control the research and restrict the participation of local residents to an advisory role during the final stages of the planning process.

Key Characteristics

Participatory action research focuses on the information and analytical needs of society's most economically, politically, and socially marginalized groups and communities, and pursues research on issues determined by the leaders of these groups. It actively involves local residents as co-investigators on an equal basis with university-trained scholars in each step of the research process, and is expected to follow a nonlinear course throughout the investigation as the problem being studied is "reframed" to accommodate new knowledge that emerges. This research generally requires the examination of a number of research questions in a serial fashion, and is best accomplished through research designs that combine quantitative and qualitative methods.

Participatory action researchers intentionally promote social learning processes that can develop the organizational, analytical, and communication skills of local leaders and their community-based organizations. They place a premium on the discovery of knowledge that can lead to immediate improvements in local conditions and are willing to act on less-than-perfect information in order to quickly address critical issues confronting the poor. They are, therefore, interested in promoting the replication of social inventions that are developed by local problem-solving teams through the widest possible dissemination in academic journals and the popular press.

Benefits

Participatory action research has provided opportunities for faculty skilled in its methods to conduct research relevant to community residents' needs while providing service learning opportunities for their students.

Involving local leaders with research enhances the problem-solving capacity of community-based organizations. By actively involving local residents in the problem-identification and definition phases of the research process, researchers reduce the possibility that the central research questions will be misidentified or ill-defined. By recruiting local residents to participate in the collection of field data, action researchers increase the number of individuals willing to share their knowledge and perceptions of the local community. Engaging local residents in the analysis of field data can minimize the number of errors in interpretation that occur when analyzing data. By actively involving residents in each step of the research process and soliciting residents' viewpoints regarding optimal solutions to local problems, researchers are more likely to identify strategies that will evoke broad-based citizen support as well as official endorsement. This increases the potential for implementation of recommendations emerging from these research efforts. By sharing control over the research process with local residents, action researchers begin to overcome the distance established by previous campus-controlled community work. Finally, by promoting social learning processes that generate considerable payoffs for both campus and community participants, community research projects are likely to be more sustainable.

Regardless of how students become involved in action research, through classes, volunteer work, or to complete the requirements for a degree, there are rich educational benefits to be acquired. In addition to learning action research methodology, they also learn about the opportunities and the dilemmas that arise with campus-community partnerships. They obtain hands-on experience working with local community leaders on the resolution of critical community concerns, thus enabling them to be more skilled and confident professionals when they enter the working world. They become more informed citizens by facing, often for the first time, the harsh realities and limited opportunities of life in very poor communities. In interdisciplinary projects, they learn to work collaboratively with other students across traditional academic boundaries.

The East St. Louis Farmers' Market

The proposal for an East St. Louis Farmers' Market emerged from a three-year-old community-university partnership involving the Winstanley/Industry Park Neighborhood Organization (WIPNO) and the University of Illinois's East St. Louis Action Research Project (ESLARP), through which faculty and students in urban planning, architecture, and landscape architecture work on community research and service projects. Community residents and university students, having successfully collaborated on the development of a comprehensive neighborhood stabilization plan for this 120-block area, worked together to complete a series of small-scale physical improvement projects. Following their renovation of an existing municipal minipark, expansion of a county-sponsored Head Start playground, and construction of a 23,000-square-foot children's play space, the members of this partnership decided to focus their efforts on activities aimed at lowering the neighborhood's high unemployment rate, which was perceived to be at the core of many of the area's most serious problems, including crime, chemical dependency, child neglect, and domestic violence.

In the fall of 1992, WIPNO recruited a small group of neighborhood residents, religious leaders, municipal officials, and university students to form an economic development task force to investigate a range of job creation strategies (Reardon, 1996). The limited success of the City of East St. Louis's externally oriented business recruitment efforts prompted WIPNO's task force members to consider various import-substitution-based economic development policies. Under an import substitution model, economic growth occurs when an expansion of local retail opportunities allows residents and institutions to purchase goods and services locally which they have previously bought outside of the community. These recaptured purchases provide direct sales to local businesses, enabling them to expand their activities and increase city revenues from local sales taxes. In the fall of 1992, the economic development task force worked with an introductory undergraduate planning class to design a household purchasing survey to determine local consumer preferences, shopping patterns, and satisfaction with products and services.

In the spring of 1993, the task force, assisted by University of Illinois students participating in a community development workshop, completed a door-to-door survey of 550 households that identified food as the largest consumer spending item in the average East St. Louis household budget. The majority of city residents surveyed had been forced to make their weekly food purchases outside of East St. Louis, and many were very dissatisfied with the product selection and prices offered by nearby suburban food stores. Over time, the task force became increasingly interested in the economic development potential of a community-owned farmers' market that would expand business and employment opportunities for East St. Louis residents while improving their access to high-quality, low-cost, farm-fresh fruits and vegetables.

In the fall of 1993, teams of local residents and students from a neighborhood planning class visited municipally operated farmers' markets in twelve Midwestern cities where the basic demographic profile mirrored that of East St. Louis. They conducted interviews with customers, vendors, and market managers regarding perceptions of their own market and the general requirements for a successful community-owned farmers' market. They learned about the importance of a central location, a low-cost structure, the variety and pricing of farm-fresh items, skillful market management, an ongoing advertising and public relations program, and attractive facilities. The results of this research led the task force to recommend the establishment by WIPNO of a community-owned and -controlled farmers' market in or near the East St. Louis central business district.

In the spring of 1994, the task force, with the assistance of a graduate planning student and faculty member, developed funding for such a facility (Whetten, 1994). The task force collaborated with three graduate architecture, landscape architecture, and urban and regional planning studios to identify the most appropriate site for the market, design an attractive yet inexpensive market structure, and secure the necessary local and state building and health permits to establish a facility where fresh foods could be sold. With the students' help, WIPNO was able to mobilize a large number of community and campus volunteers, who donated more than 43,000 hours of time to transform a long-abandoned used car lot into an attractive, open air, retail food market. When the physical rehabilitation of the market structure was completed, these graduate students helped the task force recruit fourteen local residents interested in operating stands in the new market, and worked with WIPNO to design and offer a sixteen-hour small business training program to provide would-be merchants with basic skills in purchasing, marketing, merchandising, pricing, customer relations, and accounting.

The East St. Louis Farmers' Market was opened by WIPNO on May 4, 1994, with fourteen of its forty stalls rented. Seven of the eight merchants in this first season were East St. Louis residents. The market has generated approximately $395,000 in direct sales during its 1994, 1995, and 1996 market seasons, which helped the city capture an additional $961,824 in import substitution benefits that would have, in the absence of the market, gone to suburban stores. The market has also become an important new site for community and civic activities in the East St. Louis central business district.

Research and Service Learning Outcomes

The Farmers' Market project produced significant community research and service learning outcomes during its first two years of operation. As a participatory action research project, it enabled community residents, local institutional leaders, and university students and faculty to develop a clear analysis of the city's economic problems as well as a forceful critique of its business recruitment approach to economic development. Along with the results of the household purchasing survey, this led the task force to devise an alternative economic development strategy based on the principles and methods of import substitution, resulting in the development of a local farmers' market that has generated important new business, employment, and educational and cultural benefits for local residents.

The research process pursued by the task force provided its participants with valuable participatory action research experience, which many of them have subsequently applied to a series of increasingly ambitious neighborhood improvement projects. The City of East St. Louis communicated its support for this type of community research by providing the University with $190,000 to establish a Neighborhood Technical Assistance Center, which opened in August, 1996, to offer participatory action research and other forms of technical assistance to community-based organizations involved in neighborhood improvement.

The project also provided University of Illinois undergraduate and graduate students with important service learning opportunities. Five graduate students participated as campus representatives in all phases of the task force's organizing, research, design, and development activities. In addition, three graduate studios, involving seventy-five architecture, landscape architecture, and urban and regional planning students, gained invaluable hands-on development experience assisting the task force with site selection, site planning, landscape design, building design, zoning review, building inspection, volunteer mobilization, proposal writing, physical rehabilitation, and small business training. Three students completed their master's thesis requirements by conducting a market feasibility study, devising a retail marketing and merchandising curriculum for new merchants, and evaluating alternative funding sources for the market's expansion. Over one hundred undergraduates gained valuable community outreach experience by collecting household spending data for the task force in East St. Louis's residential neighborhoods. Fifteen of these undergraduates assisted the task force in conducting field trips to a dozen successful farmers' markets sponsored by public agencies. Many additional students gained valuable experience as volunteers, working with community residents to help build the market and prepare it for its opening.

Consistent increases in the number of students enrolled in classes involving participatory research in East St. Louis, from eleven in 1990 to three hundred in 1996, demonstrate the enormous value students place on these field-based learning experiences. The large number of visits to the East St. Louis Action Research Project web site by domestic and international students also emphasizes the widespread interest these projects have stimulated.

Requirements for Successful Participatory Action Research

The farmers' market case illustrates how students from a variety of disciplines with differing levels of educational preparation were successfully involved in an ongoing participatory action research project that produced significant benefits for both community and campus participants. The case highlights the reciprocal learning that occurs in participatory action research projects in which the local knowledge of community residents is joined with the professional knowledge offered by university faculty and students to arrive at innovative solutions to community problems.

The development of similar projects on other college and university campuses will require faculty from a variety of disciplines to be trained in basic experiential education, community service learning, and participatory action research methods. To encourage faculty to participate in action research in communities requires that institutions value this emerging research methodology in promotion and tenure processes.

Local residents and leaders participating in such projects with university students and faculty must receive training in the same subject areas as the students to enable them to participate on a more equal basis. Associate degrees in organizational and community development technologies through community colleges could train residents to assume leadership positions in these projects and staff positions in community organizations that would be responsible for implementing project plans. State universities with Cooperative Extension Services might revise their Citizen Leadership and Volunteerism curricula to provide local leaders with a grounding in these subject areas.

As colleges and universities become more involved in projects in low-income areas, they must be sensitive to a number of issues. If innovative solutions emerging from participatory action research projects are not implemented in some form by local authorities, colleges and universities may become lightning rods for community protests. If, on the other hand, marginalized groups begin to receive a substantially larger share of public resources as a result of these research efforts, colleges and universities may be criticized about the redistribution of resources resulting from the empowerment process. Campus administrators must also anticipate a certain amount of political turbulence as their students and faculty become involved in controversial issues around which there may initially be little community consensus.

Finally, faculty and students must be cautious in expanding their participatory activities too quickly in a given distressed community to avoid overwhelming the small core of seasoned leaders who often hold these neighborhoods together. While we would all like to see the full range of environmental, economic, and social problems of low-income communities addressed in a holistic and systematic way in the shortest possible time, we must acknowledge the long-term disinvestment and outmigration of the past that has undermined the quality of life in these communities. The organizational capacity of primary agencies serving low-income areas requires careful, incremental development; if the process is moved along too quickly, local community leaders, on whose shoulders community revitalization rests, may become overwhelmed. Students and faculty participating in participatory action research in low-income areas can learn a great deal from the patience that indigenous leaders bring to their work as agents of social change.

References

Argyris, C., Putnam, R., and Smith, D. M. *Action Science: Concepts, Methods, and Skills for Research and Intervention.* San Francisco: Jossey-Bass, 1985.

Boyte, H. C., Booth, H., and Max, S. *Citizen Action and the New American Populism.* Philadelphia: Temple University Press, 1986.

Hall, B. "From Margins to Center: The Development and Purpose of Participatory Planning in the United States and Canada." *American Sociologist,* 1993, 23 (4), 15–28.

Meek, C. B., Nelson, R., and Whyte, W. F. "Cooperative Problem Solving in Jamestown." In W. F. Whyte and others (eds.), *Worker Participation and Ownership: Cooperative Strategies for Strengthening Local Economies.* Ithaca, N. Y.: ILR Press of the New York State School of Industrial and Labor Relations, 1983.

Reardon, K. M. *Pursuing a Local Development Strategy Based on Import Substitution: The Case of the East St. Louis Farmers' Market.* Champaign, Ill.: East St. Louis Action Research Project, 1996.

Whetten, M. K. *The Development of the East St. Louis Farmers' Market: A Community-Owned and Operated Public Market Seeking to Address the Family Nutrition and Economic Development Needs of a Low-Income Community.* Champaign, Ill.: East St. Louis Action Research Project, 1994.

Whyte, W. F. *Participatory Action Research.* Thousand Oaks, Calif.: Sage, 1991.

Whyte, W. F., Greenwood, D. J., and Lazes, P. "Participatory Action Research: Through Practice to Science in Social Research." In W. F. Whyte (ed.), *Participatory Action Research.* Thousand Oaks, Calif.: Sage, 1991.

KENNETH M. REARDON is associate professor of urban and regional planning, University of Illinois at Urbana-Champaign, where he conducts research and teaches in the fields of neighborhood planning and community development and serves as the faculty coordinator of the East St. Louis Action Research Project.

Through a review of relevant research, the authors suggest a service learning research agenda for the next five years.

A Service Learning Research Agenda for the Next Five Years

Dwight E. Giles, Jr., Janet Eyler

Research in service learning has grown rapidly over the past five years. In spite of this growth, researchers have not revised or revisited the research agenda that has been the basis for much of this research (Giles, Honnet, and Migliore, 1991). In this chapter we begin by listing the current "top ten" unanswered research questions in service learning (see Exhibit 8.1). We then review the evolution of the agenda and the progress that has been made in addressing the questions it raised. We discuss key unanswered questions in terms of outcomes related to students, faculty, institutions, community, and society. We conclude

Exhibit 8.1. The Top Ten Unanswered Questions in Service Learning Research

Students
1. How can service learning enhance subject matter learning?
2. How can we define the learning and skill outcomes that are expected in service learning?
3. What are the processes of effective service learning and how do they relate to learning in general?
Faculty
4. What factors explain faculty involvement in service learning and how are they affected by participation?
Institutions
5. How does service learning affect educational institutions, especially in regard to higher education reform?
6. What institutional policies and practices support and enhance effective service learning?
Community
7. What elements and types of community partnerships are important for effective service learning?
8. What value does service learning bring to the communities in which service takes place?
Society
9. What impact does service learning have on students' citizenship roles, community service, and other forms of social participation in later life?
10. How does service learning contribute to the development of social capital and a social ethic of caring and commitment?

by suggesting types of studies needed to advance the next phase of research in service learning.

The Top Ten Unanswered Questions in Service Learning Research

The questions in the original research agenda were the product of the Wingspread Conference convened in March 1991 by The National Society for Internships and Experiential Education (NSIEE). The conference included forty-eight participants—researchers, faculty, program directors, students, foundation executives, government officials, and national association representatives—who shared the commitment that research was needed and that a common set of questions should guide this research. Following publication of the agenda, interest and activity in service learning research increased. In 1993, for the first time, the Fund for the Improvement of Postsecondary Education (FIPSE) funded several research projects under its community service program, including our own work in the national Comparing Models of Service Learning Project. One other national study, an evaluation research study, was done by the RAND Corporation with funding from the Corporation for National Service (Gray and others, 1996). In addition there have been a number of local studies.

The obvious question in light of all of this research activity is "What have we learned?" It may be too early to make a definitive statement on all of the questions in the 1991 agenda, but we have learned that service learning can be an effective pedagogy as well as some of the conditions under which it is most effective. As the following five outcome areas illustrate, we know more about some outcomes than others.

Research About Students (Questions 1, 2, 3). Recently, the most frequently asked research questions focus on how service learning affects students. Recent findings show that service learning has a powerful impact on students' personal development, including such outcomes as sense of personal efficacy, self-esteem, confidence in political and social skills, and building relationships with others. This impact has been traced over the course of a semester (Waterman, 1993; Eyler and Giles, 1996; Kendrick, 1996) through cross-sectional data comparing service learning students with those who did not participate (Gray and others, 1996) and in qualitative studies (Ostrow, 1995; Eyler, Giles, and Schmiede, 1996; Rhoads, 1997).

An increase in social responsibility is one of the most consistent findings. Students are more likely to see themselves as connected to their community, to value service, to endorse systemic approaches to social problems, to believe that communities can solve their problems, and to have greater racial tolerance when involved in service learning (Giles and Eyler, 1994; Eyler and Giles, 1996; Markus, Howard, and King, 1993; Kendrick, 1996; Gray and others, 1996; Myers-Lipton, 1996). Although students who choose service learning show higher levels on many of these outcome measures before they undertake service, studies that attempt to isolate these predispositions from the effects of service learning have found that it has an additional independent effect (Eyler and Giles, 1996; Gray and others, 1996).

Not all studies have found this effect on personal and social outcomes (Kraft and Krug, 1994; Hudson, 1996), but this area has been so extensively explored with relatively consistent positive results that it is probably time to focus on other outcomes of service learning. The outcome of greatest interest is subject matter learning.

Most studies of subject matter learning use student self-reports of "how much is learned" rather than independent measures of outcomes for specific classes (Cohen and Kinsey, 1994; Eyler and Giles, 1996; Gray and others, 1996). One experimental study showed a modest impact of service learning on course grades (Markus, Howard, and King, 1993). A second had mixed results (Kendrick, 1996). Faculty and administrators are intensely interested in this issue, but convincing evidence of the importance of service learning to subject matter learning is still lacking.

Impact on *traditional* subject matter learning is a narrow view of expected cognitive benefits of service learning. It is quite possible that such an impact could be modest, yet that other critical cognitive outcomes such as problem solving, learning transfer, and cognitive development would be realized. One of the greatest challenges to researchers is to identify and measure appropriate learning outcomes that service learning might be uniquely designed to affect. Some exploratory work is under way to assess whether service learning contributes to complex problem analysis (Batchelder and Root, 1994), social problem-solving expertise (Eyler, Root, and Giles, in press), and reflective judgment or post-formal reasoning (Eyler, Giles, Lynch, and Gray, 1997). There is also evidence of an impact on cognitive moral development, which is a related measure of complexity of thinking about social issues (Boss, 1994). Reflective expression and ownership of knowledge also result from participation in service learning classes (Minter and Schweingruber, 1996).

To design effective programs, we need to understand how the service experience affects these outcomes. Some progress has been made in identifying program characteristics that affect the quality of service learning, many of which are consistent with the findings of Conrad and Hedin (1980) in their high school study, including the quality of the service placement, opportunities for structured reflection, and intensity and duration of the service (Eyler and Giles, 1997).

The processes that lead to learning have been less carefully studied. There is a body of qualitative literature on how students function in field settings (Shumer, 1997), and several books are available on the meaning of service (Colby and Damon, 1992; Coles, 1993; Parks Daloz, Keen, Keen, and Daloz Parks, 1996). Several attempts have been made to explore how students experience service (Ostrow, 1995; Rhoads, 1997), and one attempt to have students identify the reflective experiences most useful to them during service learning (Eyler, Giles, and Schmiede, 1996). Systematic attempts have not been made to test alternative models of reflection to ascertain which are most powerful for helping students to understand complex social issues and to work effectively in their communities. The growing field of cognitive science (Bransford and Vye, 1989), which shares many of the assumptions about learning espoused by service learning practitioners, may offer insights here. Of particular interest is the work being done with ill-structured problems (Voss, Tyler, and Yengo, 1983). Effective instruction will require systematic knowledge about how to design the students' intellectual experience with service.

Research About Faculty (Question 4). What is the impact of service learning on teaching and research? The few studies that have focused on teaching suggest that faculty value service learning for their own students' outcomes (Hesser, 1995), that their primary motivation for involvement is teaching effectiveness (Hammond, 1994), and that resistance is related to the practical difficulties of implementing programs (Driscoll, Holland, Gelmon, and Kerrigan, 1996). Institutional support is critical for faculty adoption of service learning, as Stanton (1994) has noted previously (see also Chapter Nine). The importance of faculty's role is supported by studies showing that students involved in service learning programs report closer relationships with faculty than those who are not involved (Eyler and Giles, 1996; Gray and others, 1996).

We need to understand the barriers faculty face in using service learning as pedagogy. From a qualitative study of some of the pioneers in service learning, we know that the institutions' political barriers were often more difficult to overcome than the logistical ones (Stanton, Giles, and Cruz, in press). From our involvement in faculty development workshops, we are aware of critical questions concerning how participation in service learning affects faculty careers. Specifically, these questions revolve around interdisciplinary work, promotion and tenure, and the challenges of linking scholarship in service learning to faculty careers.

Research About Institutions (Questions 5 and 6). The debate over institutionalization of service learning has often been framed as whether the effort should have marginal or mainstream status (Ehrlich, 1996). There is some indication that service learning is moving toward a more mainstream position. The Campus Compact surveys of its members indicate significant growth in the number of courses offered, and campus positions appear to be devoted to service learning. However, evidence shows that these are not highly institutionalized efforts in terms of funding or institutional priorities (Ward, 1996; Wutzdorff and Giles, 1997). Campuses that do institutionalize programs appear both to be more tightly coupled and to engage in more shared governance than those that do not (Ward, 1996). The RAND study of Learn and Serve programs reported an increase in service learning courses, although few programs offered service learning in the core curriculum. There has been a growth of service centers, though often without full-time staff and rewards for faculty and students who participate (Gray and others, 1996). Although we know that service learning options for students are increasing, we need to know whether service learning is transforming the culture of campuses and the meaning of scholarship, and we need to know what characteristics of the campus environment are conducive to service learning.

Questions about faculty and institutional involvement can be framed around the issue of higher education reform. For example, service learning practitioners often cite Boyer's (1994) work in their quest to understand how their work transforms institutions. A review of topics at recent annual conferences of the American Association for Higher Education and issues of the publication *Change* illustrates the linkage between service learning and the concerns of higher education reform. Specifically, the January–February 1997 issue of *Change* features articles such as "Higher Education and Civic Life," "John Dewey," "Educating a Committed Citizenry," and "University Community Partnerships."

Research About Community (Questions 7 and 8). A constant theme at service learning conferences has been a demand for more information about the effect of service learning on communities as well as concern for community involvement in decision making. This is ironic in that service learning espouses community partnership as a central tenet in its principles of good practice (Sigmon, 1979, 1996). There is a growing body of information about what services communities receive, including the hours served and the types of service undertaken (Gray and others, 1996; Shumer and Belbas, 1996), but there is not much evidence that service learning programs engage community members in the planning process or in the process of students' reflection about their experience (Kraft, 1996).

Research About Society (Questions 9 and 10). Any impact of service learning on society will come from the lifelong habits of citizenship and commitment that students acquire through involvement in service learning. What we know about service learning comes from studies that focus on short-term impacts, usually over the course of a semester or occasionally over a longer period such as two years (Myers-Lipton, 1996). Through moral development studies (Colby and Damon, 1992; Parks Daloz, Keen, Keen, and Daloz Parks, 1996), we are beginning to understand some of the influences that shape lives of commitment to service, community, and social justice. The finding by Rhoads (1997) that students who engage in service are more likely to personalize social concerns and are thus more willing to become involved in work for social change adds to this convergence of findings. We have some evidence for the effects of service learning on reattaching students to community service (Giles and Eyler, 1994), but long-term studies that link service learning to future participation and leadership in the community are needed to fill an important gap in our understanding.

We need to find out whether service learning can reverse the development of what McKnight (1996) has called "the careless society" and whether this form of education contributes to the long-term development of a social ethic of caring, commitment, and civic engagement.

Meeting the Research Agenda: Challenges and Directions

Having a common set of questions is a necessary step for furthering research in service learning, but that is not enough. We also need to learn more about theory, design, and gathering of data. We need consensus on the domain of service learning, and precise, measurable constructs. As in much of contemporary social science research, there is a paradigm debate in service learning about ways of knowing. "Objective" research methods are seen by many in the field as antithetical to the personal and experiential epistemology that service learning represents, whereas many skeptics see the narrative, qualitative dimensions of service learning research as anecdotal and unconvincing. We argue for a multimethod approach at this stage of service learning research. Both quantitative and qualitative methods have much to offer. In what follows we identify the types of studies that might be designed to answer the ten key questions raised in this chapter.

Matching Research Methods to Research Questions

Longitudinal studies. To understand the long-term effects of service learning upon citizenship behaviors, we need studies that follow the students participating in our programs for at least a decade beyond graduation.

Experimental studies. Because students who select service often differ from those who do not participate in service (Eyler and Giles, 1996), it is critical to test alternative models of service learning using controlled experimental designs. Such information is also important to educational policy makers.

Participatory action research. The Participatory Action Research (PAR) Model (see Chapter Seven) is beginning to emerge as a legitimate research strategy in the social sciences (Whyte, Greenwood, and Lazes, 1989). Questions of student outcomes and community involvement might best be answered by this type of design. These studies could use PAR methodology as well as historical and archival data and focus on collaborative inquiry following Sigmon's (1996) model of a reciprocal relationship in service learning.

Observational studies. The question of how the process of service learning is experienced is probably best addressed by observational studies, which have the promise of discovering the fine-grained nature of the experience of serving and learning, as illustrated by the studies of interns done by Moore (1986).

Synthesizing Research and Practice

Over the next five years it will be crucial to answer as many of the top ten questions as possible via multimethod approaches. The real challenge, however, is much bigger than that. We must understand the relationships among the various elements of the design and outcomes of service learning in its short-term and long-term effects and to integrate research and practice. In short, we need to synthesize research and practice just as service and learning are themselves integrated. Although such efforts have not yet been demonstrated, comprehensive assessment models such as the one being developed at Portland State University may point the way to a holistic approach that will overcome the shortcomings of current, fragmented research efforts (Driscoll, Holland, Gelmon, and Kerrigan, 1996).

References

Batchelder, T. H., and Root, S. "Effects of an Undergraduate Program to Integrate Academic Learning and Service." *Journal of Adolescence,* 1994, *17,* 341–356.

Boss, J. A. "The Effect of Community Service Work on the Moral Development of College Ethics Students." *Journal of Moral Education,* 1994, *23* (2), 183–198.

Boyer, E. "Creating the New American College." *Chronicle of Higher Education,* Mar. 9, 1994, p. A48.

Bransford, J., and Vye, N. "A Perspective on Cognitive Research and Its Implications for Instruction." In L. Resnick and L. Klopfer (eds.), *Toward the Thinking Curriculum: Current Cognitive Research.* Alexandria, Va.: Association for Supervision and Curriculum Development, 1989.

Cohen, J., and Kinsey, D. "'Doing Good' and Scholarship: A Service-Learning Study." *Journalism Educator,* 1994, *48* (4), 4–14.

Colby, A., and Damon, W. *Some Do Care: Contemporary Lives of Moral Commitment.* New York: Free Press, 1992.

Coles, R. *The Call of Service: A Witness to Idealism.* Boston: Houghton Mifflin, 1993.

Conrad, D., and Hedin, D. *Executive Summary of the Final Report of the Experiential Education Evaluation Project.* Center for Youth Development and Research, University of Minnesota, 1980.

Driscoll, A., Holland, B., Gelmon, S., and Kerrigan, S. "An Assessment Model for Service-Learning: Comprehensive Case Studies of Impact on Faculty, Students, Community and Institution." *Michigan Journal of Community Service Learning,* 1996, *3,* 66–71.

Ehrlich, T. "Foreword." In B. Jacoby and Associates (eds.), *Service-Learning in Higher Education.* San Francisco: Jossey-Bass, 1996.

Eyler, J., and Giles, D. E., Jr. "The Impact of Service-Learning Program Characteristics on Student Outcomes." Paper presented at National Society for Experiential Education conference, Snowbird, Utah, 1996.

Eyler, J., and Giles, D. E., Jr. "The Importance of Program Quality in Service-Learning." In A. Waterman (ed.), *Service-Learning: Applications from the Research.* Hillsdale, N.J.: Erlbaum, 1997.

Eyler, J., Giles, D. E., Jr., Lynch, C., and Gray, C. "The Impact of Different Models of Service-Learning on the Reflective Judgment of Postsecondary Students." Paper presented at the annual meeting of the American Educational Research Association, Chicago, 1997.

Eyler, J., Giles, D. E., Jr., and Schmiede, A. *A Practitioner's Guide to Reflection in Service-Learning: Student Voices and Reflections.* Washington, D.C.: Corporation for National Service, 1996.

Eyler, J., Root, S., and Giles, D. E., Jr. "Service-Learning and the Development of Expert Citizens." In R. Bringle and D. Duffey (eds.), *Collaborating with the Community: Psychology and Service-Learning.* Washington, D.C.: American Association for Higher Education, in press.

Giles, D. E., Jr., and Eyler, J. "The Impact of a College Community Service Laboratory on Students' Personal, Social, and Cognitive Outcomes." *Journal of Adolescence,* 1994, *17,* 327–339.

Giles, D. E., Jr., Honnet, E. P., and Migliore, S. (eds.). *Research Agenda for Combining Service and Learning in the 1990s.* Raleigh, N.C.: National Society for Experiential Education, 1991.

Gray, M. J., Feschwind, S., Ondaatje, E. H., Robyn, A., Klein, S., Sax, L., Astin, A. W., and Astin, H. S. *Evaluation of Learn and Serve America, Higher Education: First Year Report.* Vol. 1. Santa Monica, Calif.: RAND Corporation, 1996.

Hammond, C. "Integrating Service and Academic Study: Faculty Motivation and Satisfaction in Michigan Higher Education." *Michigan Journal of Community Service Learning,* 1994, *1,* 21–28.

Hesser, G. "Faculty Assessment of Student Learning: Outcomes Attributed to Service-Learning and Evidence of Changes in Faculty Attitudes About Experiential Education." *Michigan Journal of Community Service Learning,* 1995, *2,* 33–42.

Hudson, W. E. "Combining Community Service and the Study of American Public Policy." *Michigan Journal of Community Service Learning,* 1996, *3,* 82–91.

Kendrick, J. R., Jr. "Outcomes of Service-Learning in an Introduction to Sociology Course." *Michigan Journal of Community Service Learning,* 1996, *3,* 72–81.

Kraft, R. J. "Service Learning." *Education and Urban Society,* 1996, *28* (2), 131–159.

Kraft, R. J., and Krug, J. "Review of Research and Evaluation on Service Learning in Public and Higher Education." In R. Kraft and M. Swadener (eds.), *Building Community: Service Learning in the Academic Disciplines*. Denver: Colorado Campus Compact, 1994.

Markus, G. B., Howard, J. P. F., and King, D. C. "Integrating Community Service and Classroom Instruction Enhances Learning: Results from an Experiment." *Educational Evaluation and Policy Analysis*, 1993, *15* (4), 410–419.

McKnight, J. *The Careless Society: Community and Its Counterfeits*. New York: Basic Books, 1996.

Minter, D. W., and Schweingruber, H. "The Instructional Challenge of Community Service Learning." *Michigan Journal of Community Service Learning*, 1996, *3*, 92–102.

Moore, D. T. "Knowledge at Work: An Approach to Learning by Interns." In K. Borman and J. Reisman (eds.), *Becoming a Worker*. Norwood, N.J.: Ablex, 1986.

Myers-Lipton, S. "Effect of a Comprehensive Service Program on College Students' Level of Modern Racism." *Michigan Journal of Community Service Learning*, *3*, 1996, 44–54.

Ostrow, J. "Self-Consciousness and Social Position: On College Students Changing Their Minds About the Homeless." *Qualitative Sociology*, 1995, *18* (4), 357–375.

Parks Daloz, S., Keen, C. H., Keen, J. P., and Daloz Parks, L. A. *Common Fire: Lives of Commitment in a Complex World*. Boston: Beacon Press, 1996.

Rhoads, R. A. *Community Service and Higher Learning: Explorations of the Caring Self*. Albany: State University of New York Press, 1997.

Shumer, R. "What We've Learned from Qualitative Research." In A. Waterman (ed.), *Service-Learning: Applications from the Research*. Hillsdale, N.J.: Erlbaum, 1997.

Shumer, R., and Belbas, B. "What We Know About Service Learning." *Education and Urban Society*, 1996, *28* (2), 208–223.

Sigmon, R. "Service-Learning: Three Principles." *Synergist*, 1979, *8*, 9–11.

Sigmon, R. *Journey to Service-Learning*. Washington, D.C.: Council of Independent Colleges, 1996.

Stanton, T. "The Experience of Faculty Participants in an Instructional Development Seminar on Service-Learning." *Michigan Journal of Community Service Learning*, 1994, *1*, 7–20.

Stanton, T., Giles, D. E., Jr., and Cruz, N. *To Strengthen Service-Learning Policy and Practice: Stories from Early Pioneers*. San Francisco: Jossey-Bass, in press.

Voss, J., Tyler, S., and Yengo, L. "Individual Differences in Social Science Problem Solving." In R. Dillon and R. Schmeck (eds.), *Individual Differences in Cognitive Processes*. Vol. 1. New York: Academic Press, 1983.

Ward, K. "Service-Learning and Student Volunteerism: Reflections on Institutional Commitment." *Michigan Journal of Community Service Learning*, 1996, *3*, 55–65.

Waterman, A. "Conducting Research on Reflective Activities in Service-Learning." In H. Silcox (ed.), *A How-to Guide to Reflection: Adding Cognitive Learning to Community Service Programs*. Philadelphia: Brighton Press, 1993.

Whyte, W., Greenwood, D., and Lazes, P. "Participatory Action Research." *American Behavioral Scientists*, 1989, *32* (5), 513–551.

Wutzdorff, T., and Giles, D. E., Jr. "Service-Learning in Higher Education." In J. Schine (ed.), *The 97th Yearbook of the National Society for the Study of Education*. Chicago: National Society for the Study of Education, 1997.

DWIGHT E. GILES, JR., is professor of the practice of human and organizational development and director of internships at Peabody College, Vanderbilt University.

JANET EYLER is associate professor of the practice of education at Peabody College, Vanderbilt University.

DWIGHT E. GILES, JR., and JANET EYLER are co-principal investigators on a national service learning research project, funded by FIPSE, on comparing models of service learning in higher education. They recently completed a study of students' views of reflection activities in service learning for the Corporation for National Service.

Successful integration of service learning in higher education hinges on addressing organizational culture and faculty roles and rewards.

Addressing Academic Culture: Service Learning, Organizations, and Faculty Work

Kelly Ward

"Service" is mentioned in a majority of college and university mission statements, but how its meaning translates into campus life varies considerably. For many campuses, service often means membership on committees that contribute to the institution or a faculty member's professional affiliations. On other campuses, such as Michigan State University, service tends to be defined as faculty professional outreach, such as consulting in the field in ways that call on the faculty member's scholarly expertise. On other campuses, such as Salish Kootenai College, a tribal college in Pablo, Montana, service means direct service to students and the reservation community surrounding the campus; faculty engage in efforts that benefit the community by offering their professional expertise; students participate in both curricular and co-curricular activities to meet community needs.

Clearly, these are all different interpretations of service. Now with the advent of discussions about service within the context of undergraduate education, the following new questions are being raised: What does service learning mean? Where does it fit organizationally? What implications does it have for faculty work? Responses to these questions hinge upon the culture of the institution and its faculty.

University missions are translated through symbols and systems, particularly the curriculum and faculty reward structures. The curriculum conveys what faculty identify as important to teaching and learning. The curricular integration of service learning indicates that an institution values service to the community as part of the educational experience. At Portland State University, for example, there are formalized opportunities in the curriculum for students to address the needs of the local urban community in classes ranging from art to biology. Portland State interprets service as community problem solving and sends a clear message that the university is actively involved in the life of the local community. Accordingly, at Portland State, service learning has been incorporated into faculty promotion and tenure policies.

Faculty reward structures also signal institutional values. Faculty success at the organizational level, translated as promotion and tenure, requires faculty participation in the tripartite demands of the professoriate: teaching, research, and service. These demands on faculty time vary a great deal, depending on the particular campus culture. If a campus values experiential learning and community involvement, it will value professors who utilize service learning; if it is recognized and rewarded in promotion and tenure guidelines and reviews, professors will be encouraged to incorporate service learning into their courses.

Organizational Culture: Expanding Horizons for Service Learning

If we are to realize the ideals suggested in this issue of *New Directions for Teaching and Learning* and look to the future for more widespread use of service learning, we must consider the context within which academically based service takes place. Innovations in higher education must be assimilated into the institution or they will be short-lived (Curry, 1992). The institutionalization of service learning requires garnering support from people throughout the campus community and involves the following challenges: (1) administrative support, (2) familiarity with course-based service, (3) funding, and (4) faculty involvement. Moving service learning from the periphery to the core, and from an idea to practice, requires addressing these challenges while understanding the complexities of the organizational context and faculty work.

Administrative Support. Many campuses have benefited from the involvement and support for service learning from senior administrators, particularly presidents. For example, Campus Compact, an organization of college and university presidents, is now over 500 campuses strong. The Compact's popularity among senior administrators is in part attributed to how service learning responds to many of the criticisms currently leveled against higher education, including the failure to meet public service responsibilities (Boyer, 1990; Fairweather, 1996). Presidents and other senior-level administrators look to service learning to smooth relationships with their constituencies and to better prepare students for life beyond college.

Service learning depends not only on the support of senior-level administrators, but on other administrators as well. An expanded administrative vision includes involvement of those directly and actively involved in routine academic management and policy functions (that is, provosts, deans, department chairs). These administrators can promote service learning by creating and supporting an ethos of learning that includes community service experiences. This may be accomplished by amending promotion and tenure policies to include service learning and by articulating a vision of community service to their academic units (Kuh, Douglas, Lund, and Ramin-Gyurnek, 1994).

Familiarity with Course-Based Service. The reality is that much variance exists with regard to campus awareness of service learning. On some campuses service learning is a term familiar to a majority of the campus community. At Western Montana College, for example, the chancellor has been supportive of service learning by creating the Center for Service Learning and by integrating service into the campus mission statement. She has also hosted a campuswide convocation on community service and experiential learning in addition to several faculty workshops on the topic. Service learning has also been a theme at faculty orientation for two years, and about one-third of the faculty have a service component in their courses. Faculty use service learning as a pedagogical tool, and students understand that emphasis is placed on out-of-class work.

In contrast, service learning at Montana State University is still in an introductory phase. Faculty and students are increasingly involved in service learning, but interest and participation exist only in small pockets across the campus. The Office for Community Involvement is gaining visibility, but it takes time and multiple efforts to make service learning familiar campuswide. The president, though supportive, is not actively involved in promoting service learning on campus.

Funding. Service learning, like all other endeavors on a campus, requires adequate funding. Financial and human resources are necessary to create and staff offices to support service learning and to support faculty efforts and service projects. Based on a review of campuses involved in Campus Compact's Project on Integrating Service with Academic Study, Morton and Troppe (1996) outline eight common steps for institutionalizing service. Among the steps they cite, five relate to funding: (1) institutional commitment of funds to ensure the development of the service learning initiative, (2) a staff person to serve as a liaison between faculty and community agencies, (3) faculty development funds to introduce faculty to service learning, (4) support of faculty travel to find out how others in their discipline and on similar campuses have implemented service learning, and (5) release time for faculty to redesign their courses to incorporate service learning.

In a series of case studies of campuses in Montana integrating service learning, faculty and administrators indicated the importance of funding of both individual projects and campus offices as reflections of institutional priorities. One mid-level administrator explained, "We can't say service learning is an important part of the college and then not put resources in to make it work." Simply put, funding allocations signify institutional priorities. An example is the creation and expansion of an office to support service learning and volunteerism. Such an office is essential to advance awareness and promote participation in curricular-based service. An actual location for service learning activities communicates to the campus that the initiative is valued. Further, a campus office is a structural means to provide information to the community, both on and off campus. Service learning administrators provide a crucial link between students, faculty, and the local community.

Faculty Involvement. One of the greatest challenges facing the widespread adoption of service learning is faculty involvement. Faculty are the arbiters of the curriculum, and service learning as a curricular initiative needs both their support and participation. Most campuses utilize a system of shared governance and make decisions via committees. Therefore, it is imperative that committees dealing with curricular issues be challenged by deans and department chairs to consider service learning and how it might be included in promotion and tenure guidelines.

The University of Utah provides an example of how faculty involvement in the advancement of service learning has been used to transform campus culture. The Lowell Bennion Community Service Center involves thousands of students in service each year. The Center has an academic senate–approved Service Learning Scholars Program for students to acknowledge their involvement in service, and several programs for faculty release time and other awards to recognize those experienced and new to service learning. Further, the faculty advisory committee that works with the Bennion Center has drafted guidelines to help departments include service learning in their promotion and tenure policies (Lowell Bennion Center, 1996).

Many factors have shaped the success of the Bennion Center. Presidential leadership was important, but perhaps even more so was the central role that faculty played in shaping policies and also reaping the benefits of such policies through reward structures. For service learning to be integrated into campus culture, as exemplified at the University of Utah, it must move from a hazy notion often perceived by faculty as additional unrewarded work to a valued and recognized endeavor.

Expanded administrative support, increasing familiarity of the campus community, funding, and faculty involvement in service learning are all crucial to the success of academic-based service on any campus. Perhaps the greatest challenge to service learning, however, is the nature of faculty work and the faculty reward structure. The challenge lies in faculty reluctance to participate in work that is not recognized and rewarded by their institution. The institutionalization of service learning cannot be addressed without discussing faculty work and rewards.

Faculty Work and Rewards

Faculty roles are shaped by the academic department as well as by institutional culture and mission. For example, at Salish Kootenai College, service learning is a curriculum requirement and faculty are recognized for their involvement. The campus focuses on teaching and service, and faculty commitments are centered locally. Faculty are expected to serve both the campus and the local community. In contrast, at Pennsylvania State University, the mission of the institution and faculty work is centered around research and scholarship. Consequently, the vast majority of Penn State faculty devote significant portions of their time to research and writing. This is not to say that all the faculty at Salish Kootenai College are involved in service learning and none are at Penn State. The point is that differences exist between the two schools because of their reward structures. Nonetheless, some faculty at Penn State will be motivated to use service learning independent of their concerns for promotion and tenure or because they can directly tie service learning to their scholarly endeavors.

As the preceding examples illustrate, faculty work varies considerably. Faculty identify with aspects of their institutions in differing degrees. Some faculty are more focused on their department than their campus; others see their discipline as their primary affiliation; and still others see the university or college as the core unit of identification (Clark, 1987; Kuh and Whitt, 1988; Tierney and Rhoads, 1993). All of these sources of professional identity may influence one's willingness to use service learning pedagogies.

For many faculty there is increasing emphasis on research, and rewards tend disproportionately to favor excellence in research (including grant procurement) over teaching and service regardless of institutional type (Boyer, 1990; Fairweather, 1993, 1996). Although service learning has the potential to enhance teaching, research, *and* service, it is still largely viewed by faculty as a service or instructional initiative. The faculty member who feels research is the focus of the reward structure may steer away from service learning. Consequently, specific guidelines stressing service learning as a component of promotion and tenure are needed. For example, the University of Utah provides criteria that departments can use to evaluate faculty involved in service learning. These standards offer direction to departments wanting formally to evaluate and validate involvement in service learning. The following are examples of these criteria:

- Service learning contributions must relate to the faculty member's area of scholarship.
- Service learning contributions are responsive to recognized needs of individuals and organizations within the university or local community and are seen as having lasting impact.
- The service learning activities provide a means for students to synthesize their volunteer experiences with course content (action and reflection).

Faculty participation in meaningful and academically relevant service is key to expanding involvement in community-based learning. Clearly, faculty involvement in service hinges upon being rewarded and supported for their efforts. In fact, any initiative centered around teaching or service is bound to fail if faculty are not given recognition for time they spend on these activities and time they spend with students. The campus that purports to support involvement in service learning, but then fails to recognize these efforts in faculty rewards, will not be able to attract large or even small numbers of faculty to this initiative. This is akin to the argument offered by Tierney and Bensimon (1996) when they pointed to the importance of having promotion and tenure guidelines correspond with institutional priorities.

The institution with a vision for more widespread use of service learning must consider the policies and procedures that directly influence faculty work. Institutional leaders who support service learning need to do so not only with words, but with actions as well. To be sure, presidents, provosts, vice presidents, and deans do not have absolute power. They do, however, have the ability to create offices of service learning, voice their support for faculty involvement in service, and earmark funds for faculty development and project support.

Negotiating Culture: Overcoming Barriers and Resistance to Change

The following strategies are suggested for faculty and administrators involved in advancing service learning on their campuses.

Make sure that all administrators—presidents, provosts, vice presidents, deans, department chairs—are familiar with campus service learning initiatives. One of the major barriers to incorporating service learning is lack of familiarity. Many people are simply unaware of academic-based service and its benefits. To garner support from all levels of the university requires familiarity within each unit.

Change takes place slowly and incrementally; try to influence culture at all levels. Service learning hinges on the involvement of all levels of the campus—students, staff, faculty, and administrators. These groups need first to be introduced to service learning and then kept apprised of strides in this area. Make the accomplishments of course-based service known to all members of the campus community.

Create formal and informal faculty committees and groups to help direct the efforts of service learning. Collegial decision-making through committees and groups is the norm on most college campuses. Influencing culture requires utilizing decision-making norms to make policy about the curriculum, faculty roles, and the future of service learning on campus. A service learning committee can help create policies for service learning and can also influence other committees (for example, executive committees of the faculty senate, faculty development committees). A service learning interest group is also essential to spreading the language of service—an important cultural artifact—to all domains of campus.

Service learning is undoubtedly related to other university-based initiatives; tie into them. Higher education is facing a time in which faculty and administrators are challenged to do more with less. Service learning certainly has merits on its own, but it can also benefit by connecting with other related initiatives.

For example, if an institution has an undergraduate research program, look at ways to do community-based action research (see Chapter Seven) to meet the goals of both service learning and research.

Work with faculty senates and curriculum committees to stress the academic side of service learning. Service learning is a component of the curriculum, and the way to influence the curriculum is through the faculty. Some faculty are reluctant to acknowledge service learning as a viable academic pedagogy because words like *service* can conjure up images of learning that might be "soft" or "fuzzy" and perceived as tangential to the undergraduate experience. Campus members need to be educated about service learning's role in furthering academic course objectives.

Address faculty reward structures, for they mirror institutional priorities. Faculty rewards are essential to the ongoing integration and growth of service learning. Introduce the language of service learning into promotion and tenure guidelines. This may mean starting with departments that are service learning friendly and then expanding campuswide.

Provide data about benefits of service learning. Faculty are concerned with the intellectual rigor of curricular initiatives. Influencing culture requires speaking the language, and academics tend to converse around research and evaluation. Providing research-based evidence about the benefits of service learning is useful to sway the reluctant faculty member. Research outcomes can be drawn from both national and institutional-based studies (Boss, 1994; Giles and Eyler, 1994; Markus, Howard, and King, 1993; RAND Corporation, 1996).

Integrating Service Learning

The ideas and suggestions put forth in this chapter are meant to contribute to the institutionalization of service learning on campus. If service learning is not integrated into campus cultures through infrastructure (for example, service learning offices, institutional budgets), faculty reward structures, and curricular affairs, it is destined to be short-lived (Rhoads, 1997).

The late Ernest Boyer was one of service learning's champions. He called for a new conception of faculty work and a new vision of scholarship: "One dedicated not only to the renewal of the academy but, ultimately, to the renewal of society itself" (Boyer, 1990, p.81). Boyer's wisdom can be honored by realizing the potential of service learning to help reshape the future of teaching and learning in higher education.

References

Boss, J. A. "The Effect of Community Service Work on the Moral Development of College Ethics Students." *Journal of Moral Education,* 1994, *23* (2), 183–198.

Boyer, E. *Scholarship Reconsidered: Priorities of the Professoriate.* Princeton: Carnegie Foundation for the Advancement of Teaching, 1990.

Clark, B. R. *The Academic Profession.* Berkeley: University of California Press, 1987.

Curry, B. K. *Instituting Enduring Innovations: Achieving Continuity of Change in Higher Educa-tion.* ASHE-ERIC Higher Education Report No. 7. Washington, D.C.: School of Educa-tion and Human Development, George Washington University, 1992.

Fairweather, J. S. "Academic Values and Faculty Rewards." *Review of Higher Education,* 1993, *17,* 43–68.

Fairweather, J. S. *Faculty Work and Public Trust: Restoring the Value of Teaching and Public Service in American Academic Life.* Needham Heights, Mass.: Allyn & Bacon, 1996.

Giles, D. E., and Eyler, J. "The Impact of a College Community Service Laboratory on Stu-dents' Personal, Social, and Cognitive Outcomes." *Journal of Adolescence,* 1994, *17,* 327–339.

Kuh, G. D., Douglas, K. B., Lund. J. P., and Ramin-Gyurnek, J. *Student Learning Outside the Classroom: Transcending Artificial Boundaries.* ASHE-ERIC Higher Education Report No. 8. Washington, D.C.: George Washington University, 1994.

Kuh, G. D. and Whitt, E. J. *The Invisible Tapestry: Culture in American Colleges and Universi-ties.* ASHE-ERIC Higher Education Report No. 1. Washington, D.C.: George Washing-ton University, 1988.

Lowell Bennion Center. *Service Learning in the Curriculum.* Salt Lake City: University of Utah, 1996.

Markus, G. B., Howard, J.P.F., and King, D. C. "Integrating Community Service and Class-room Instruction Enhances Learning: Results from an Experiment." *Educational Evalua-tion and Policy Analysis,* 1993, *15* (4), 410–419.

Morton, K., and Troppe, M. "From the Margin to the Mainstream: Campus Compact's Proj-ect on Integrating Service with Academic Study." In M. Troppe (ed.), *Two Cases of Insti-tutionalizing Service Learning: How Campus Climate Affects the Change Process.* Providence, R.I.: Campus Compact, 1996.

RAND Corporation. *Evaluation of Learn and Serve America, Higher Education: First Year Report.* Vol. 1. Santa Monica, Calif.: RAND Corporation, 1996.

Rhoads, R. A. *Community Service and Higher Learning: Explorations of the Caring Self.* Albany: State University of New York Press, 1997.

Tierney, W. G., and Bensimon, E. M. *Promotion and Tenure: Community and Socialization in Academe.* Albany: State University of New York Press, 1996.

Tierney, W. G., and Rhoads, R. A. *Faculty Socialization as Cultural Process: A Mirror of Insti-tutional Commitment.* ASHE-ERIC Higher Education Report No. 93–6. Washington, D.C.: George Washington University, 1993.

KELLY WARD *is director of Volunteer Action Services—the campus center for service learning and volunteerism—at the University of Montana and assistant professor of higher education in the Department of Educational Leadership.*

Service learning challenges the faculty practitioner with its complexity relative to traditional classroom practice. The conceptual matrix in this chapter attempts to render that complexity more transparent.

A Service Learning Approach to Faculty Development

Edward Zlotkowski

The Resource Book, compiled by the Massachusetts and Maine Campus Compacts for the June 1996 New England Regional Institute on Integrating Service with Academic Study, represents more than the sum of its parts. Included in the volume are essays with titles like "From Teaching to Learning—A New Paradigm for Undergraduate Education," "Bowling Alone: America's Declining Social Capital," and "The New Scholarship Requires a New Epistemology." None of these pieces is directly concerned with service learning; in fact, they hardly mention it. Instead, they concern themselves with broad social and educational trends—the context within which service learning must be understood and developed if it is to flourish (Zlotkowski, 1995; 1996).

The chapters in this volume, *Academic Service Learning: A Pedagogy of Action and Reflection,* may, at first glance, seem to fall into an entirely different category. After all, they have been brought together precisely because each of them deliberately and explicitly explores service learning. Yet, in a more subtle way, they point to the same conclusion as the pieces referenced above. The survival of service learning, as well as its significance, rests on the interplay of factors and concerns not often brought into close proximity: academic expertise and social commitment; disciplinary methodology and community empowerment; epistemological, civic, and logistical considerations side by side. Indeed, unlike other educational reform initiatives, service learning seems determined not to throw the baby out with the bath water and also not to waste any more bath water than is absolutely necessary! Thus, rather than suggesting that greater social involvement will compensate for less academic rigor, service learning maintains that enhanced academic effectiveness is one of its most important benefits. Nor should one be tempted to see in its hands-on activities a neglect of theory: in its baggage, service learning packs a whole wardrobe of theoretical and epistemological challenges to the status quo. On the other hand, even staples of traditional education such as the lecture-discussion are not so much denied and discarded as they are re-contextualized.

Thus, the problem at hand: How can service learning practitioners best understand its conceptual richness, best sort out and arrange its constituent elements, so that they can go about steadily increasing their competence rather than succumbing to a sense of inadequacy? Without wishing to imply I have already navigated this dangerous passage myself, I would nonetheless like to suggest one approach to mapping—clearly and comprehensively—the main areas of concern that make up this enterprise.

Toward the beginning of the 1995–1996 academic year, I set about trying to bring whatever service learning experience and expertise I had acquired as director of Bentley College's Service Learning Project to a new appointment as a senior associate at the American Association for Higher Education (AAHE). I found myself in a very particular bind. One of my new responsibilities was to help others within AAHE relate service learning to their own areas of educational expertise, yet all my work up to that point had been, so to speak, from the inside looking out. What I needed now was some heuristic device that would help me explain to my new colleagues—and to myself—the bigger picture; namely, how and where I saw service learning interfacing with other, for the most part, far more established institutional concerns. To this end, I eventually developed the matrix shown in Figure 10.1.

Figure 10.1. Service Learning Conceptual Matrix

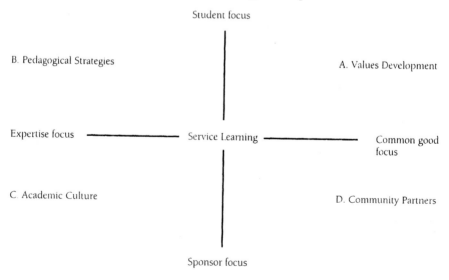

Student focus

B. Pedagogical Strategies

A. Values Development

Expertise focus ——————— Service Learning ——————— Common good focus

C. Academic Culture

D. Community Partners

Sponsor focus

General Features of the Matrix

The central structural feature of the matrix, two intersecting axes, is familiar. Unlike many other matrices of this sort, however, the axes here do not so much serve to indicate the *relative* position of some particular with regard to two coordinates as they do to help conceptualize service learning as falling into one (or more) of four general areas.

A second important feature of the matrix is its emphatically educational perspective. Even at a glance, one cannot help but note the seemingly uneven distribution of quadrants between academy concerns (A through C) and community concerns (D). Such a seeming imbalance demands some explanation.

Few topics in service learning have excited more interest—or passion—than the relative importance of academy and community concerns in framing the service learning enterprise. Whereas some focus heavily on its ability to promote tangible community benefits, others see its value much more closely tied to gains occurring in and through the academy's traditional educational mission.

The matrix presented here either mediates or evades this tension, depending on one's point of view. On the one hand, it does indeed privilege academic concerns. It presupposes that the academy and the programs it supports are, first and foremost, defined by an educational agenda; that is, generating knowledge and facilitating learning. On the other hand, it also insists that the very thing that makes service learning distinctive is its willingness to admit community concerns (quadrant D) as one of the academy's *essential* responsibilities. Thus, from a service learning perspective, the academy itself must be defined as including, in all sectors, a community dimension.

Indeed, over and beyond its graphic insistence that quadrant D, community partners, forms an essential part of the academy's work—having points at which that quadrant directly abuts the more overtly academic quadrants—the matrix also suggests that each of the other quadrants likewise bears directly on its neighbors. Thus, "values" (quadrant A) not only interfaces with "community" but also with "pedagogy" (quadrant B) and "academic culture" (quadrant C). The same can be said for "pedagogy" and "academic culture" in their relationship to the other quadrants.

What does this mean in practice, and why should it matter to the individual service learning practitioner? It means, in the first place, that no matter how tempting it may be to see service learning merely as a set of pedagogical practices linking specific students with specific underserved communities, in point of fact such connections ultimately depend on a much larger, much more complex educational undertaking. This, in turn, implies that the more we can bring a broader sense of integrity to our service learning work, the stronger and more skillful our specific practices will become. Conversely, the more we limit our understanding of service learning to classroom practice, ignoring, for example, the need to ground it in theory, research, and discipline-specific scholarship (quadrant C), the more vulnerable our actual practice will be to both intellectual attack and institutional neglect.

One other general feature of the matrix deserves some attention. The *horizontal axis*—that spanning academic expertise and a concern for the common good—suggests the observation that a failure to locate one's work with regard to both poles will leave one either vulnerable to professional attack or ineffective in promoting civic awareness. At the same time, the *student–sponsor axis* suggests the importance of a different kind of balance; in this case, that between classroom- or student-based concerns and those of other stakeholders. The latter include not only community partners but also the various units into which the academy is organized. Thus, pedagogical excellence—with regard both to specific course content (quadrant *B*) and larger civic or social issues (quadrant *A*)—satisfies only one set of stakeholders, students, and even the addition of community partners still leaves a third critical constituency out of account. Indeed, unless we are willing to see departments, divisions, our institutions in their entirety as another set of essential stakeholders whose needs we are obliged to take into account, it is hard to see how we can legitimately demand their assistance and recognition. This being the case, an essential part of our work must involve the careful documentation and monitoring of service learning activities, dialogue with sponsoring administrative units on how service learning can meet *their* needs, and outreach to colleagues in our field.

The Four Quadrants

We turn now to the contents of the four quadrants, noting that these brief discussions are meant to be illustrative rather than comprehensive. Indeed, as the other essays in this volume indicate, almost every one of the topics referenced in the four quadrants deserves its own individual treatment.

Values Development. We begin where service learning itself may be said to begin—with a concern for values, awareness, and social engagement. Within quadrant *A*, we should include not only topics such as citizenship education (see Chapter Four) and multiculturalism (see Chapter Five) but also many of those concerns that have typically been assigned—or abandoned— to student affairs; for example, ethical and professional responsibility, peace and justice issues, leadership development, and the American tradition of service to the community. Service learning asks faculty to assume a sense of ownership for all these issues, regardless of individual expertise. Such ownership does not, of course, imply every faculty member every time. Just as most faculty work out of a specific disciplinary focus, so most service learning practitioners will naturally gravitate more toward one of these values-related areas than the others.

To incorporate such concerns successfully in one's teaching while maintaining a discipline-specific base requires careful planning and genuine skill in facilitating reflection. Since most faculty possess little experience in this area, the concerns of quadrant *A* offer an excellent opportunity for meaningful collaboration among faculty and student affairs personnel, community partners, and service learning student leaders. Indeed, when one surveys the large number of colleges and universities that utilize student leaders in their programs, the single most common student function may be assisting faculty with reflection.

Nonetheless, as the inclusion of some of these concerns in this volume testifies, the work of quadrant A must never be thought of as anything other than an integral part of a faculty-guided undertaking. The fact that values development has most often been associated with student affairs is undoubtedly one of the main reasons that so many institutions assign service learning program development to student affairs personnel. These individuals, sometimes with little institutional power and limited familiarity with faculty culture, face an almost insurmountable task in developing and retaining faculty interest.

Pedagogical Strategies. If Values Development represents the soul or spirit of service learning, Pedagogical Strategies represents its heart—the organ that keeps it alive, that allows its spirit to take concrete form. Like Values Development, Pedagogical Strategies encompasses many different kinds of interests and initiatives. Experiential education, collaborative learning, critical thinking, undergraduate research, and action research (see Chapter Seven) all represent pedagogical models that readily lend themselves to service learning appropriation and development. However, as Chapter Three makes clear, the bottom line for service learning as a pedagogy—regardless of the specific practices it draws on—is active learning. Active learning, in turn, helps transform the faculty role from "expert witness" to project designer or facilitator. Such a role demands that service learning practitioners make several key decisions.

Perhaps the most important of these relates to the most appropriate way to frame the service experience. Implementation of theory, testing of theory, developing problem-framing and problem-solving skills, providing a "real world" connection, broadening and deepening the moral imagination—all represent legitimate ways to frame the service experience from an academic perspective. The appropriateness of the perspective chosen will frequently be a direct function of the discipline in which the service work is embedded. The general reluctance of literature teachers to embrace service learning probably stems less from personal indifference than from the mistaken notion that only the disciplines that develop practical skills or test social theory can legitimately utilize this approach. That a genuine understanding of literature depends to no small extent on one's ability to appropriate it imaginatively, and that such appropriation can be powerfully enhanced by broadening a student's experiential base, could provide this group of faculty with a much more suitable approach to service learning than has, up until now, been the case.

Another key strategic decision concerns how service learning is formally structured into a course. Should it, for example, be mandatory or elective, short-term or long-term, individual or group? How one answers these questions will depend not only on the nature and goals of the course in question but also on the personal circumstances that define both instructor and students. Thus, an instructor with little service learning experience may opt to limit its role in a course until he or she feels more confident about knowing what to do and what to expect. Analogously, a class made up largely of older, working students with family obligations may necessitate making the service component only one of several equally weighted options from which students may choose.

Other important decisions relate to one's choice of reflection tools (for example, journals, focus groups, integrative essays) and assessment strategies (for example, pretests and posttests, interviews, portfolios, supervisor evaluations). By now, excellent models exist for almost all of these, and in building their competence, faculty should take advantage of the many resources already available. This is especially true with regard to disciplinary base. Over the last year, there has been a major increase in the quantity and the quality of discipline-specific service learning studies (for example, Cooper and Julier, 1995; Ender and others, 1996). By the end of 1997, over half a dozen discipline-specific service learning monographs will have been published by the American Association for Higher Education in areas as diverse as composition and accounting, nursing and political science. Since each of these volumes contains theoretical essays and bibliographical materials as well as model courses and programs, they should contribute to a new level of sophistication and effectiveness in service learning pedagogy.

Academic Culture. Just as "reflection" spans both Values Development and Pedagogical Strategies, so discipline-specific studies belong both to Pedagogical Strategies and to Academic Culture. Earlier in this essay, I indicated that one of the concepts the matrix suggests is a far more coherent approach to faculty responsibilities than is currently the norm. However, if most service learning advocates would readily concede a critical connection between values and pedagogy, a much smaller number would concede an equally critical connection between pedagogy and academic culture, the concern of quadrant C. Indeed, for many service learning faculty, quadrant C, the first quadrant so far *not* directly concerned with student development—moral, civic, or cognitive—hardly enters the picture, except as a source of concern or complaint.

This is unfortunate. For within this quadrant, we find represented issues such as faculty roles and rewards, definitions of scholarship, faculty professional service, departmental and disciplinary cultures, and institutional citizenship. And although one might protest that such concerns reflect precisely the kind of academic orientation service learning seeks to deemphasize, such a reaction would be short-sighted if not suicidal. After all, how much time and space service learning practitioners have to devote to moral, civic, or social concerns is largely a function of what happens in quadrant C. Thus, while it is true that some faculty will continue to pursue such concerns regardless of the professional consequences, most faculty very much need a framework of disciplinary legitimacy and institutional support if they are to devote themselves seriously to a service learning pedagogy.

What, then, are the tasks that Academic Culture demands of service learning faculty? First, faculty need to continue to amass intellectual capital through research and scholarship. Studies of the philosophical traditions in which service learning is grounded (see Chapter Two), of service learning impacts (see Chapter Eight), of the movement's epistemological implications (Liu, 1995;

Richman, 1996) contribute to this process. Second, as already mentioned, they need to pay far more attention to the professional contexts where they work; that is, the disciplines and departments that define and reward them (Zlotkowski, 1995; 1996). Third, they need to press their institutions to honor the service dimension of their mission statements in a coherent, comprehensive manner, ensuring that agendas on all levels—divisional, departmental, and individual—contribute fully to that goal (see Chapter Nine).

Community Partners. Up until now, faculty responsibilities as described by the matrix have all focused on traditional constituencies: students, colleagues, academic units. As the name Community Partners implies, Quadrant D takes us beyond those constituencies into a sphere of activity foreign to most faculty. To be sure, collaboration with community partners is already implied in the student-anchored work of quadrants A and B. Thus, insofar as collaboration is needed either to facilitate effective reflection or to ensure the success of academic projects, community partners have been a part of the matrix from the very beginning. What is at issue here, however, is not how community partners can assist the work of the *academy* but rather how the academy can facilitate the work of *community partners*.

This being the case, perhaps the most elementary—and important—faculty responsibility in quadrant D is to ensure that service learning arrangements are genuinely reciprocal and that the community's needs are not subordinated or sacrificed to academic objectives. When such an imbalance develops, however unintentionally, service learning becomes but one more chapter in the already long history of the academy's exploitation of the community for its own ends (see Chapter Seven).

Taking responsibility to see that this does not happen probably implies more direct faculty contact than may be necessary for purely academic success. It may even involve a faculty member's willingness to provide service himself or herself—a form of outreach based on professional expertise, not general good will (Lynton, 1995). Naturally, one important side benefit of such extended engagement is the opportunity to develop a service-based scholarship agenda of one's own.

There is still another way of taking responsibility for the needs of community partners, a way that goes beyond personal service, however important that service may be. In his essay "The Irony of Service: Charity, Project, and Social Change in Service Learning," Keith Morton (1995) explores what it means to move from a "thin" to a "thick" notion of partnership: "My observations suggest that there exist a series of related but distinct community service paradigms that I will refer to as charity, project and transformation. Each paradigm . . . contains a world view, a problem statement and an agenda for change. Each paradigm has 'thin' versions that are disempowering and hollow, and 'thick' versions that are sustaining and potentially revolutionary" (p. 24). Building on this distinction between "thick" and "thin," one can identify a variety of ways in which service learning faculty can help "thicken" the collaborations they form. By taking the time to understand the bigger picture that defines a community organization's priorities, faculty can utilize their insider status to make still other university resources available: colleagues willing to sponsor projects of their own; compensation for staff who supervise students and facilitate reflection activities; access to technical assistance, libraries, computer labs, and training sessions; opportunities to take, or at least to audit, cost-free courses that upgrade important skills—these are just a few of the ways in which faculty can support the community's own agenda, apart from the requirements of a particular service learning project.

In short, the situation here, in this second *sponsor focus* quadrant, is not dissimilar to what we found in quadrant C. The work of the service learning practitioner is not just a matter of designing and implementing successful courses. It *naturally* involves broader concerns—the transformation of academic culture and the creation of a more dynamic relationship between that culture and "civic culture" (Boyer, 1990).

Conclusion

Whatever the validity and value of the matrix I have described, it seems to me incontestable that efforts to make service learning a more effective educational strategy cannot succeed unless practitioners come to pay detailed attention to all four of the areas represented in the matrix. That this will be a challenge cannot be denied, especially since the entire right side of the matrix, the *common good focus,* has received so little attention for so many years. For that very reason, some may be tempted to overcompensate, treating issues of academic culture and disciplinary expertise with benign neglect. But willful mistakes of our own cannot undo the mistakes of the past. All essays in this volume testify to the intrinsic complexity of service learning as an educational undertaking. Out of this complexity grows the true potential of academic service learning.

References

Boyer, E. L. *Scholarship Reconsidered: Priorities of the Professoriate.* Princeton, N.J.: Carnegie Foundation for the Advancement of Teaching, 1990.

Cooper, D. D., and Julier, L. (eds.). *Writing in the Public Interest: Service Learning and the Writing Classroom:* East Lansing: Michigan State University, 1995.

Ender, M. G., and others (eds.). *Service Learning and Undergraduate Sociology: Syllabi and Instructional Materials.* Washington, D.C.: American Sociological Association, 1996.

Liu, G. "Knowledge, Foundations, and Discourse: Philosophical Support for Service Learning." *Michigan Journal of Community Service Learning,* 1995, 2 (1), 5–18.

Lynton, E. A. *Making the Case for Professional Service.* Washington, D.C.: American Association for Higher Education, 1995.

Morton, K. "The Irony of Service: Charity, Project, and Social Change in Service Learning." *Michigan Journal of Community Service Learning,* 1995, 2 (1), 19–32.

Richman, K. "Epistemology, Communities, and Experts: A Response to Goodwin Liu." *Michigan Journal of Community Service Learning,* 1996, 3 (1), 5–12.

Zlotkowski, E. "Does Service Learning Have a Future?" *Michigan Journal of Community Service Learning,* 1995, 2 (1), 123–133.

Zlotkowski, E. "A New Voice at the Table? Linking Service Learning and the Academy." *Change,* 1996, 28 (1), 20–27.

EDWARD ZLOTKOWSKI is founder of the Service Learning Project and professor of English at Bentley College. He currently serves as a senior associate at the American Association for Higher Education, where he directs the monograph series on service learning and the academic disciplines.

Key resources for the field of service learning include books, journals, and a web site designed to help practitioners and researchers.

Resources for Research and Practice in Service Learning

D. Scott Dixon

With calls for greater accountability on the part of external stakeholders, American higher education has been forced to take a fresh look at its academic mission. Increasingly, more educators have called for "critically reflective learning" and the need to engage students in "a continual process of activity, reflection upon activity, [and the] collaborative analysis of activity" (Brookfield, 1986, p. 10). Equating learning with experience and reflection is not new, nor is it confined to the American educational system. Dewey (1916) called on teachers to engage learners in continuous and alternating experiences of investigation and exploration followed by reflection, and Freire (1970) equated the idea of "praxis" with the goal of not only helping South America's poor acquire literacy skills but also to use such skills to understand and resist oppressive social structures.

One way this emphasis on learning and experience has manifested itself has been the desire to connect the classroom with the community through service learning. As Thomas Ehrlich, former chair of Campus Compact, wrote: "Service learning is the various pedagogies that link community service and academic study so that each strengthens the other" (Jacoby, 1996, p. xi).

This chapter provides some key resources for researchers, practitioners, administrators, and teachers who are interested in further exploration into the world of service learning.

Web Site

The following web site organized by the Corporation for National Service allows Internet searches on the current uses and resources of service learning within the academy: http://www.cns.gov/links.htm#servicelearning.

Books

Janet Eyler, Dwight E. Giles, Jr., and Angela Schmiede, *A Practitioner's Guide to Reflection in Service-Learning: Student Voices and Reflection.* Nashville, Tenn.: Vanderbilt University, 1996.

This research-based publication examines students' experiences of critical reflection. It is an interactive workbook that supplements the more theoretical work within service learning by providing a practical resource to developing reflective activities for service learning courses, programs, and other forms of experience-based education. By using comments from students involved in service learning and providing creative ideas to help students reflect on their service learning experiences, this book addresses the following objectives: to use service learning in classes and programs; to convince colleagues and administrators of the value of service learning; to discover what students value about service learning; to develop varied instructional activities around service learning; to adapt activities for students with diverse learning styles; to sequence reflective activities within class; and to identify other resources for planning service learning classes and reflection activities.

Barbara Jacoby and Associates, *Service-Learning in Higher Education: Concepts and Practices.* San Francisco: Jossey-Bass, 1996.

The authors' theoretical framework situates service learning within the larger realm of educational outcomes of the academy. Multiple audiences include senior administrators who need to discover the value of service learning; academicians who need to understand how service learning contributes to teaching, learning, and research; faculty who are unaware of the many ways service learning can be integrated into courses across the curriculum; student affairs professionals who desire more opportunities to design service learning activities that foster student development; student leaders who want to incorporate reflection and reciprocity into the implementation of their campus programs; community leaders who need to be informed about the mutually beneficent partnerships available within service learning projects; and policy makers who need to be reminded of how important their support can be to an institution dedicated to promoting service learning.

Robert A. Rhoads, *Community Service and Higher Learning: Explorations of the Caring Self.* Albany: State University of New York Press, 1997.

Hoping to restructure higher learning around a more caring and democratic form of education, the author presents community service as one possible vehicle for transforming the academy toward an ethic-of-care philosophy. Rhoads links actual service projects and interviews with over one hundred students to theoretical research on the "self" and "community" in order to demonstrate how community service offers a vivid encounter between the "self" and the "other." Ultimately, Rhoads uses his argument to present a new conception of service learning called "critical community service," which combines a feminist ethic of care with a democratic concern for social justice and equality.

Alan S. Waterman (ed.), *Service-Learning: Applications from the Research.* Hillsdale, N.J.: Erlbaum, 1997.

Waterman and associates bring together the work of leading researchers in the field of service learning to accomplish two primary objectives: first, to review and evaluate the empirical research; and second, to generate recommendations gained from this literature to be used in the planning and implementation of service learning programs. The first part of the book discusses qualitative and quantitative methodologies that have been used to assess service learning programs. The second portion of the volume discusses the elements of effective service learning programs, including characteristics of the programs themselves, variables affecting teaching involvement, and student motivations. The book concludes with a chapter written from a practitioner's perspective that attempts to draw together the common themes presented in the book and reiterate the many recommendations offered by its contributors.

Edward Zlotkowski (ed.), AAHE's Series on Service Learning in the Disciplines. Washington, D.C.: American Association for Higher Education, 1997–1998.

Each of eighteen volumes in this series provides a rigorous intellectual forum for discussion of why and how service learning is being implemented within a specific discipline, and what that discipline is contributing to the pedagogy of service learning. Each volume consists of theoretical and pedagogical essays by scholars in the discipline as well as an annotated bibliography and program/course descriptions.

Journals

Michigan Journal of Community Service Learning, OCSL Press, University of Michigan, 1024 Hill Street, Ann Arbor, Michigan 48109–3310; http://www.umich.edu/~ocsl/MJCSL/. Contact: Jeffrey Howard, Editor.
Journal of College Student Development, Student Development Office, Appalachian State University, Boone, North Carolina 28608; http://www.jcsd.appstate.edu/. Contact: Gregory S. Blimling, Editor.

References

Brookfield, S. D. *Understanding and Facilitating Adult Learning.* San Francisco: Jossey-Bass, 1986.
Dewey, J. *Democracy and Education.* New York: Macmillan, 1916.
Freire, P. *Pedagogy of the Oppressed.* New York: Continuum, 1970.

Jacoby, B., and Associates. *Service-Learning in Higher Education: Concepts and Practices.* San Francisco: Jossey-Bass, 1996.

D. SCOTT DIXON *is assistant professor in the Department of Biblical Studies at Cedarville College.*

INDEX

Academic culture: faculty responsibilities and, 86–87; faculty support and, 86. *See also* Organizational culture

Academic service learning. *See* Service learning

Accountability, higher education, 91

Action research: Lewin's ideas on, 18; as service learning pedagogy, 85

Administration, service learning programs and, 74–75

Administrators, educating, 78

Alinsky, S., 58

American Association for Higher Education (AAHE), 69, 82, 86

American culture: careless society and, 69; consumerism vs. citizenship in, 3; critiques of, 3; education's role in, 3; family values and, 3; individualism vs. community in, 3; service learning and, 3–4. *See also* Society

American Jewish Congress, 18

American Philosophical Society for Promoting Useful Knowledge, 14

Argyris, C., 58, 44

Aristotle, 33

Assessment strategies, 86

Astin, A. W., 4

Bacon, F., 12–13, 18

Banking model, 5

Barber, B., 33

Batchelder, T. H., 67

Beidelman, W., 28

Belbas, B., 69

Belenky, M. F., 42

Bellah, R. N., 1, 3

Bender, T., 14

Bensimon, E. M., 40, 41

Benson, L., 12, 13, 14, 16

Bentley College, 82

Booth, H., 58

Boss, J. A., 67, 79

Boud, D., 52

Box, I., 13

Boyer, E. L., 1, 4, 18, 69, 74, 77, 79, 88

Boyte, H. C., 58

Bransford, J., 68

Bringle, R. G., 28

Brookfield, S. D., 91

Butts, R. F., 12

Campus Compact, 68, 74–75, 81, 91

Campus Outreach Support League (COOL), 5

Cary, E., 14

Change, 69

Change agents: indigenous leaders as, 64; students as, 40, 69

Chesler, M. A., 23

Chicago Pragmatism, 17

Citizenship, 3, 69

Citizenship education: in America, 34; definition of, 34–35; Democracy Project and, 34–35; democratic education and, 34–35; service learning and, 32, 34–35, 37–38, 69, 84

Citizenship Schools, 4

Clark, B. R., 77

Classroom: lecture format in, 28; transformation of, 25–26. *See also* Synergistic classroom

Clinchy, B. M., 42

Cognitive moral development, 67

Cognitive processes, reflective thinking and, 52

Cognitive science, 68

Cohen, J., 67

Colby, A., 67, 69

Coles, R., 1, 40, 44, 67

Collaborative learning, 85

Columbia University, 14–15, 17

Commission on Community Interrelations (CCI), 18

Community, research on, 69 critical multiculturalism and, 44; cultural difference and, 44; service learning and, 37

Community partners. *See* Community-campus partnerships

Community service: D.C. project and, 44; recovering lost connection through, 44; self-other linkages and, 92–93

Community-based learning: definition of, 6; Dewey's contribution to, 17; faculty participation and, 77; service learning and, 6. *See also* Democracy Project (Swarthmore)

95

ORDERING INFORMATION

NEW DIRECTIONS FOR TEACHING AND LEARNING is a series of paperback books that presents ideas and techniques for improving college teaching, based both on the practical expertise of seasoned instructors and on the latest research findings of educational and psychological researchers. Books in the series are published quarterly in Spring, Summer, Fall, and Winter and are available for purchase by subscription as well as by single copy.

SUBSCRIPTIONS cost $54.00 for individuals (a savings of 35 percent over single-copy prices) and $90.00 for institutions, agencies, and libraries. Please do not send institutional checks for personal subscriptions. Standing orders are accepted. Prices subject to change. (For subscriptions outside of North America, add $7.00 for shipping via surface mail or $25.00 for air mail. Orders must be prepaid in U.S. dollars by check drawn on a U.S. bank or charged to VISA, MasterCard, or American Express.)

SINGLE COPIES cost $22.00 plus shipping (see below) when payment accompanies order. California, New Jersey, New York, and Washington, D.C., residents please include appropriate sales tax. Canadian residents add GST and any local taxes. Billed orders will be charged shipping and handling. No billed shipments to post office boxes. (Orders from outside North America must be prepaid in U.S. dollars by check drawn on a U.S. bank or charged to VISA, MasterCard, or American Express.)

SHIPPING (SINGLE COPIES ONLY): $30.00 and under, add $5.50; to $50.00, add $6.50; to $75.00, add $7.50; to $100.00, add $9.00; to $150.00, add $10.00.

DISCOUNTS FOR QUANTITY ORDERS are available. Please write to the address below for information.

ALL ORDERS must include either the name of an individual or an official purchase order number. Please submit your order as follows:
   Subscriptions: specify series and year subscription is to begin
   Single copies: include individual title code (such as TL54)

MAIL ORDERS TO:
   Jossey-Bass Publishers
   350 Sansome Street
   San Francisco, CA 94104–1342

PHONE subscription or single-copy orders toll-free at (888) 378–2537 or at (415) 433–1767 (toll call).

FAX orders toll-free to: (800) 605–2665

FOR SUBSCRIPTION SALES OUTSIDE OF THE UNITED STATES, CONTACT:
any international subscription agency or Jossey-Bass directly.

OTHER TITLES AVAILABLE IN THE
NEW DIRECTIONS FOR TEACHING AND LEARNING SERIES
Robert J. Menges, Editor-in-Chief
Marilla D. Svinicki, Associate Editor